GLORY GLORY MAN UNITED!

MY YEARS AT OLD TRAFFORD

GLORY GLORY MAN UNITED!

BRYAN ROBSON
with
MARTIN CHILTON

CollinsWillow

An Imprint of HarperCollins*Publishers*

First published in 1992 by
Collins Willow
an imprint of HarperCollins Publishers
London

© Brown Packaging Ltd 1992

Brown Packaging asserts the moral right to
be identified as the author of this work

A CIP catalogue record for this book is
available from the British Library

ISBN 0 00 218434 6

Editorial and production by Brown Packaging Ltd
Design by Allister Cordice Design Ltd

Printed and bound in Great Britain by
Severn Valley Press Ltd

ACKNOWLEDGEMENTS

I wish to thank Michael Phelan and Archie Knox for
their co-operation. I am particularly grateful to
Tommy Docherty and Ron Atkinson, who were
generous with their time. Appreciation should also be
extended to Duncan Carmichael, David Mason,
Dunfermline Athletic FC, the Football Association
and to Barney Chilton, for his help with the statistics.
I am also indebted to Theresa McDonald, for access
to her collection of material on Manchester United.

My thanks also to Ashley Brown, for his helpful
comments on the text, to Michael Doggart of
CollinsWillow and to Harry Swales.

Martin Chilton

BIBLIOGRAPHY

Frankly Speaking by Frank Stapleton, published by
Blackwater Press in 1991
Manchester United: The Quest For Glory 1966-91 by
Tommy Docherty (with Martin Chilton), published
by Sidgwick & Jackson in 1991
Soccer At The Top by Matt Busby, published by
Weidenfield and Nicholson in 1973.
Sparky: Barcelona, Bayern & Back by Mark Hughes
(with Peter Fitton), published by Cockerel Books Ltd
in 1989
Strachan Style: A Life In Football by Gordon Strachan
(with Ken Gallacher), published by Mainstream
Publishing in 1991

PICTURE ACKNOWLEDGMENTS

The publishers would like to express their particular
thanks to Bob Thomas Sports Photography for their
kind permission to reproduce the following pictures
in this book: title page, front cover top right, top
centre and bottom left, back cover bottom right, and
on pages 5, 7, 8, 10, 12, 13, 16, 20, 21, 22, 24, 29, 30
[all], 32, 34, 36, 37, 39, 40, 41, 44, 45, 46, 47, 48,
50, 51, 52, 53, 54/55, 60, 61, 62, 64, 66, 67, 70
[both], 71, 72, 73 [both], 74, 76, 77, 78, 79, 80, 81,
82, 86, 88, 89, 90/91, 93, 96, 98/99, 102, 103, 105,
106, 108, 109, 112/113, 114, 115, 116, 119.

Thanks also to the following picture agencies and
libraries:
Colorsport, for the illustrations on the front cover top
left and bottom centre, back cover top, bottom left
and bottom right and on pages 11, 18, 19, 42, 56, 58,
63, 69, 83, 84, 95/96 [both], 97, 100, 101, 110;
Associated Sports Photography for the picture on
pages 68/69; Syndication International for the
illustrations on pages 26 and 38; and finally to Rex
Features for the picture on page 15.
Title page: Bryan Robson celebrates his goal in the
1990 FA Cup semi-final. **Front cover:** United
manager Alex Ferguson (top left); United's Cup
Winners' Cup team of 1991 (top centre); Robson
with the FA Cup (top right); Ryan Giggs in action
(bottom left); United's League Cup winners with the
trophy at Wembley in 1992 (bottom centre); and the
Reds' Danish goalkeeper Peter Schmeichel (bottom
right). **Back cover:** the 1985 FA Cup-winning team
collect the Cup (top); Robson injured (bottom left);
in action (bottom right) and in action with Paul Ince
during the 1991 League Cup Final (bottom centre).

In action for Manchester United against Montpellier, in the quarter-final of the European Cup Winners' Cup in 1991.

CONTENTS

PREFACE

I arrived at Old Trafford in October 1981, yet it only seems like yesterday. Signing for Manchester United is a move I have never regretted, and I have enjoyed my first 11 seasons of high drama with the greatest club in football. A few disappointments have been far outweighed by the rewarding times, the countless memorable matches, the pleasure of being able to play alongside world-class team-mates and trophies I have lifted. The highlights of my career have been shared with supporters I regard as the finest in the game.

I have always looked ahead to the next challenge, but I welcome this chance to look back over my momentous years with Manchester United. It is a satisfying feeling, because I can honestly say that I have enjoyed my career to the full.

This book could not have been written without the help of many of my former team-mates, managers and people within the club and the game. I should like to thank them all for their time and memories during its completion.

Finally, I would like to add my particular thanks to Martin Chilton, for writing, editing and producing the final manuscript.

THE GREATEST CLUB

The first time I stepped out on to the pitch at Old Trafford in that famous red shirt was one of the proudest moments of my life. There is simply nothing to match the grandeur and charisma of the most famous football club in the world. The glorious stadium buzzes with expectation, and it is easy to understand why one of United's greatest heroes, Bobby Charlton, described the ground as 'the theatre of dreams'.

Manchester United Football Club has a unique, glorious history and every player who signs for the club knows that great things are expected of him. During my 11 years at Old Trafford I have gathered a treasure of great memories, but even though I have achieved so many of my ambitions, there are good reasons to be optimistic about the future that is in store for United, and I intend to be part of the challenge to establish the club as the best in Europe — and that quest for glory begins afresh in the new Premier League in the 1992-93 season.

Although we were pipped at the post for the League Championship in the 1991-92 season, it had still been a momentous nine months for the Reds — during which we had won the Football League Cup for the first time in United's history, and lifted the European Super Cup, the only occasion the club has won that trophy. The 1992 League Cup triumph came a year after the team had won the European Cup Winners' Cup and two years after victory over Crystal Palace in the 1990 FA Cup Final.

The father of Manchester United

In May 1992 Manchester United also secured the FA Youth Cup for a record seventh time. The Youth Cup had been absent from the Old Trafford trophy cupboard since George Best and his talented young team-mates had last won it in 1964, and the reappearance of that coveted trophy is proof that the club's youth system is in the best condition it has been in since the reign of Sir Matt Busby.

The current players have certainly proved that there is more to United than its illustrious past but, that said, no other club in the world can boast the special history of United. Most of the credit for its brilliant reputation is due to Matt Busby. He is the father of Manchester United. In 1945 he took over a debt-ridden club, which did not even have its own ground then, and built it into the most successful in Britain. Within four years United had won the FA

George Best, here scoring against Sheffield Wednesday at Old Trafford, was the finest British player ever.

Cup, beating Blackpool in 1948, and had finished as First Division runners-up three years in a row.

Uniquely for the time, Busby had demanded and won complete autonomy over the team. His ideas about how the game should be played were fresh and influential, and I have been told that he was the first tracksuit manager; something which is commonplace in football today, but was special then, when most managers did not go near the training ground. 'The ball is made round to go round, so keep passing it and playing football and results are bound to come,' was the basis of Busby's message for nearly a quarter of a century. His concepts may appear simple, but his teams played football that was beautiful in a way nothing in British football has ever equalled. He could coax brilliant performances from players, even stars, because they wanted to impress him. George Best, the player whose skill he admired above all others, still refers to Busby as a 'superhuman being'.

In the 1950s he rebuilt United and in the process developed one of the greatest sides in the history of the game. The 'Busby Babes', as they were dubbed, reared by Matt and his shrewd right-hand man, Jimmy Murphy, won the new FA Youth Cup in 53, 54, 55, 56 and 57. I have spoken to many people at United who recall seeing the Babes play, and they are full of praise for those awe-inspiring lads. The Babes side that won the League in 1956, by a remarkable margin of 11 points, had an average age of 21.

These youngsters were set to dominate European football for years, but the club's dream was shattered in the most tragic fashion on 6th February 1958 in the Munich Air Crash. On that fateful day, eight players — Roger Byrne, Geoffrey Bent, Eddie Colman, Mark Jones, David Pegg, Tommy Taylor, Billy Whelan and Duncan Edwards, who died later in hospital from his injuries — three club officials, eight journalists and other members of the party returning from a successful European Cup tie in Belgrade perished on the runway at Munich. The plane had stopped to refuel and crashed on take-off, on an icy runway, at the third attempt .

Busby himself suffered injuries so severe that he was given the Last Rites, but being a born fighter he pulled himself back from death's door. The tragedy had a profound influence on the club, and football fans all over the world. As Bobby Charlton, one of the Babes who survived the crash, put it: 'Before Munich it was Manchester's club. Afterwards, everyone felt they owned a little bit of it.'

At a stroke, Busby lost the bulk of a team whose potential knew no bounds and, naturally, it took a long time to put the club back on its feet. While Busby and Murphy were rebuilding, United had some miserable seasons. In 1962-63 United finished 19th in Division One, avoiding relegation only by the skin of their teeth. Yet the club's enduring spirit helped it rise from the ashes, and the loyalty of the fans, something that has remained a constant source of strength right up to the present, was cemented.

Below: **Denis Law, the 'King' of Old Trafford, waltzes past West Ham's Bobby Moore. Law scored 236 goals in 399 appearances for Manchester United.**

Right: **Denis Law with, to his right, George Best, David Sadler and Bobby Charlton. Law is holding aloft the League Championship trophy on 13th May 1967, the last time the title has come back to Old Trafford. United claimed the trophy in real style that season, winning 17 and drawing four of their 21 matches at home, and they did not lose a single League game after their defeat against Sheffield United on Boxing Day 1966. Since then, the failure to bring back the title has grown into an obsession with the fans. United finished second in 1968, and again under Dave Sexton in 1980, and during my 11 years at Old Trafford, United have twice finished as runners-up. To emulate Law and company, and win the title with United, would be a dream come true.**

With a new crop of players, most homegrown and a few bought, Busby brought some silverware back to United in 1963. That FA Cup Final win against Leicester marked the beginning of another burst of success, and it was the most glorious of Busby's reign. When Denis Law, signed from Torino for a record £115,000, scored on that joyous Wembley day, United signalled that they were a club reborn.

To most of United's fans the Busby Babes are just celebrated names in the annals of the club's history, but many older fans, or their parents, have vivid memories of the great teams Busby assembled in the 1960s. I, myself, went to see his 1960s side a few times with my dad, Brian — I was named after him, but my parents used the 'y' instead of an 'i'. The first time I saw them was against Sunderland. Although I was a Newcastle fan at that time, we made a special trip to Roker Park to see the famous Red Devils.

Watching the Busby legends

In September 1965, when I was nearly nine, my dad took me to see Manchester United, who were then the reigning champions, at St James's Park. Newcastle United had just returned to Division One after winning the Second Division title. In front of 57,380 enthralled fans, Busby's team won 2-1, with goals from David Herd and Denis Law. The greats were in action that day: Best, Charlton, Stiles, Brennan, Dunne, Crerand — and Herd and Law, of course. Even to a young lad it was clear just how exciting and skilful they were. It is no surprise that they scored 84 goals in 42 League games that season.

That 1964-65 team had been the first United side to capture the League for eight seasons, and the achievement is still recalled with affection by people at Old Trafford. During the battle for supremacy with Howard Wilkinson's Leeds United in 1991-92, a few people reminded me that Manchester United had edged the title in 1965 just ahead of Leeds. Although both clubs had finished with 61 points, the Reds had won the championship because they had a better goal average than Don Revie's Leeds. Sadly, history did not repeat itself 27 years later!

Within two seasons the title was back at Old Trafford. The 1966-67 season had gone according to Busby's plan — win at home and try to get at least a point away — a cast-iron method for success under the system of two points for a win. United were unbeaten at home and undefeated in their last 20 games. They claimed the title by winning 6-1 at West Ham, typical of the brilliant way they had played throughout the campaign. Best said: 'If the title had been decided on home games we would have won it every season, but in 1966-67 our away performances made the difference.' Over a million people watched United's home games, the highest number since the War. Unfortunately, it has so far proved to be the last time that the title has come back to Old Trafford.

In the 1967-68 season United finished as runners-up to neighbours Manchester City, but the club's energies that season had been devoted to winning the European Cup — a challenge Busby had described as: 'The quest for the Holy Grail'. That crusade, which had been gripping the club for the decade after Munich, came to its climax on 29th May 1968 in a never-to-be forgotten Final against Benfica, who had the great Eusebio in their team, at Wembley.

Above: **Matt Busby, the father of Manchester United. Winning the European Cup had been Busby's ultimate ambition and in 1968, 10 years after the Munich crash, he achieved his dream.**

With the game poised at 1-1 after 90 minutes and the players waiting on the pitch before extra time, Busby showed why he was such an inspirational manager. I have been told by some of the players just how drained they felt, yet they were given great heart by Busby, who strode on to the pitch looking completely composed. He went round to each player and quietly encouraged him, preaching his usual advice about keeping possession with accurate passing. With renewed zeal, the team went on the rampage in extra time, scoring three marvellous goals, and helping to fulfil Busby's personal dream.

Today's fans get great enjoyment from occasionally speculating on the qualities of that team of the late 1960s. A good measure of their brilliance is that they are the only team in Britain ever to have had three current European Footballers of the Year in their line-up. Law had won the award in 1964, Charlton in 1966 and Best in 1968. What a trio.

Whenever I meet these three favourite sons I am struck by their abiding love for the club. Charlton, in particular, who played an astonishing 754 first-team games for the club, lives and breathes Manchester United. What a privilege it must have been to play in the same team as them. Law had razor-sharp reflexes and his goalscoring skills were as fine as they come. He netted 236 goals in 399 games for the Reds.

George Best was simply a class apart. You can legitimately talk in the same breath about whether Best or Pele was the greatest player the game has ever produced. If you asked 500 people in a room which one they would select, the vote would probably be split 250 for each.

That European Cup victory remains the most glorious chapter in the club's history. United, the first English team to play in Europe, had become the first English club to win the Champions' Cup. That European dream is something we want to recreate at the club, and this is why winning the League Championship is so important — it is the only route in to compete for the Champions' Cup, which is the ultimate test for any European club.

'Creating my own nursery'

Matt Busby's eyes have lit up whenever he has talked to me about the game against Benfica. He has remained a colossal figure at the club. In my time at United I have been to numerous social functions with him and have the greatest respect for the man, not just because of his dazzling achievements, but because he is a deeply compassionate, dignified person, who has time for everyone he meets. In over a decade of acquaintance I have never heard him utter a bad word about anyone. He has sometimes told me that he likes a particular player, but if he has had any criticism of the team, or individual players, it has not been passed on. Whenever he has talked about the game I have listened attentively, because it is like having one of the most learned professors offering you advice about his subject. He knew what it was all about and obviously possessed enough granite in his character to have mastered others, but without a degree of hardness, he would never have been such a successful manager.

In recent years some of the men who played under him have returned to the club. Bobby Charlton has been a director since 1984, and Brian Kidd, Jim Ryan and Nobby Stiles are part of Alex Ferguson's backroom team. Whenever I have talked to them about what is was like to play for Matt Busby, they have all described him with the utmost affection. They respect his knowledge of the game, and they cherish his kindness to them as people.

Eight of the players who did Matt proud that May night in 1968 were products of the club's youth policy. 'That victory against Benfica proved that my dreams of creating my own nursery for footballers had come true,' Sir Matt once told me. He had been adamant from the moment he joined United that the surest road to success is a policy of nurturing as many talented homegrown players as possible. His assistant Jimmy Murphy used to refer to the youth policy as developing an orchard and he took great pride when another 'golden apple', as he called a trainee, was 'ripe' for the first team.

This emphasis on youth has stayed with the club. Throughout the 1970s splendid players, including Sammy McIlroy, Arthur Albiston and Andy Ritchie, came through the juniors; and in the 1980s Clayton

Blackmore, Mark Hughes and Norman Whiteside all progressed from the ranks. It has not been possible to have a continuous stream of exceptional players breaking through, and there have been lean periods, but in Alex Ferguson's reign this is an aspect of the club that is flourishing again.

The FA Youth Cup, which had been regarded in Busby's time as being almost as important as the championship, was won by Manchester United in 1992 for the first time in 28 years, and a whole crop of talented youngsters has come through. In 1992, the PFA 'Young Player of the Year' trophy was awarded to an Old Trafford player for the second year running, the only time a club has achieved this feat. Ryan Giggs, the teenage winner in 1992, is the discovery of the decade. He is the brilliant emblem of United's revitalised youth system and he is certain to become one of the all-time greats. Although his predecessor for the PFA award, Lee Sharpe, was bought from Torquay, he came to United when he was only 17 and learned his trade here.

Those players who progress from the club's own creche always manage to get a bit closer to the hearts of United's fanatical supporters, because the fans love to see players who have done well for the club in the Lancashire League and in the Reserves come through and make it at the highest level for the Reds. The fans seem to appreciate them all the more because they haven't been bought for a lot of money. I would loved to have come up through the youth system at United. I enjoyed my apprenticeship at West Bromwich Albion, but I don't think there

would have been anything to match following in the footsteps of Edwards, Charlton and Best. Ironically, however, when I was just a lad, playing for Chester-le-Street junior schools team, I had about 13 clubs, including Arsenal, Leeds and Newcastle, trying to sign me on schoolboy forms — but Manchester United weren't one of them!

Youngsters have to be spotted before they can be signed and Alex Ferguson has done a superb job revitalising the scouting system at the club. At the start of the 1990s he hired one of my old heroes, and namesake, Bryan 'Pop' Robson, to organise the club's scouting system in the northeast, and he later promoted him to work at the club. It boosted my morale no end, too, as to avoid confusion I am now known at Old Trafford as the *young* Bryan Robson!

Alex Ferguson believes that youth players are paramount to his long-term plans for success, and he has employed several former players to organise the youth policy. Having ex-United players involved, including European Cup-winning stars Brian Kidd and Nobby Stiles, has definitely strengthened that aspect of the club. Their love of the club is contagious, and they can instill it in impressionable youngsters. Once the lads have been discovered, then Eric Harrison, the youth team coach, does a first-class job in developing their skills and teaching them good habits. He tries to get them to play football in

Below: **Tommy Docherty and Stuart Pearson hold aloft the FA Cup in 1977, while Gordon Hill and Sammy McIlroy, far left, salute the crowd.**

the right way, ensuring that their apprenticeship at Old Trafford will provide them with the right kind of grounding, however far they go in the game.

The benefit of having former United players on the staff is that they understand the special demands that young players at the club face nowadays — and there is no more difficult place to learn your trade, because of the strain you are under. But any young lad who has chosen to try and make it as a professional footballer relishes the challenge of making the grade and loves playing the game for a living. There is surely a lot more pressure on a youngster who has left school and is forced to sign on the dole.

This is not to deny that there are great expectations placed on players at Old Trafford, even very young ones, and any United player soon realises that he has to be successful to survive here. Manchester United is not a home for losers. As an apprentice at West Brom, I definitely had an easier time than youngsters here face, because at the Hawthorns we were granted a bit of breathing space to develop. There was less of a search for perfection and you could get on with learning your trade away from any glare of publicity. This is true of most English clubs.

The unique appeal of United

United's youth system did go downhill in the years immediately following Busby's retirement in April 1969, at the age of 58. If anything, the demands on the players and the new manager were fuelled and not released by Busby's decision to quit. He left a momentous legacy. He had won the European Cup, the League Championship five times — finishing as runners-up a further seven times — won the FA Cup twice, and reached the Final on two other occasions.

Busby decided that he had accomplished all there was to achieve. For his successor, the legacy proved to be a real albatross. The supporters still demanded glittering trophies, yet the people who would have to bring them were fast running out of time and inspiration, as Bobby Charlton later commented: 'Winning the European Cup in 1968 was the greatest moment Manchester United has had, but it was never quite the same after. The players had strived so long to win that particular prize that our ambitions after were an anticlimax.'

Now, in the 1990s, players find it strange to be asked to emulate United's legends, and people such as Bobby and Nobby Stiles, so closely involved with United, act as a constant reminder of the past. Wherever you go at Old Trafford you can see that the club is saturated in its history. There are countless reminders of the club's wonderful past. Names such as Duncan Edwards and George Best seem to hang in the air. Even young supporters, who weren't even born when Best was rifling in goals for United, still live and breathe memories of these sensational stars. Wherever we play, the players can hear United's fans celebrating the great stars of the past. Interspersed with chants honouring Mark Hughes, myself, Paul Ince and Steve Bruce, will be songs about the Busby Babes and Best. There is no other club in Britain

where the past crowds the present to such an extent. United's supporters are quick to compare players and teams with those of yesteryear and the fans expect nothing but the best.

This heritage can be viewed as a heavy burden, but for me it is part of the unique appeal of the club and it amounts to a challenge I have actually relished. Without the celebrated past there would not be a legacy of fantastic support, and United's fans are the best in the world. Performing in front of 45,000 or more fans at every home game is the dream of most professional footballers, but it is something that Manchester United players can count on.

United's supporters have remained steadfast even through bad years. The fans do expect a lot, but as long as players try their best, the crowd will always stick by them. Supporters might criticise someone during a bad performance, but once the game is over, their loyalty is unquestioned. That dedication is one of the main reasons I have enjoyed living in the Manchester area, because my relationship with the fans is important to me.

In the past two decades, however, some United players have not regarded living up to these demands as a challenge. They have felt intimidated or haunted by the club's golden image and have buckled under the pressure of this tremendous expectation. Many of the players who have admitted finding it hard to adjust are those who have arrived from small clubs. United's players have to be able to cope with being under a global spotlight. It is not just the thousands who come to Old Trafford, it is the millions of fans all around the world who have great expectations.

Docherty's flying wingers

The pressure on players at United has grown steadily since Busby stepped down. Things started to go wrong for the club in the early 1970s. The years just after his retirement were not happy ones for United. His chosen successor was Wilf McGuinness, a former United player, who had a brief, turbulent spell in the job. He led the club to three domestic Cup semi-finals, but he was inexperienced in management — and only in his early 30s — and ran into difficulties supervising the players, many of whom were former team-mates and friends. He later admitted that he had trouble emulating Busby: 'I should have been stronger, but I was in awe of him.'

McGuinness was sacked in December 1970 and with him went Busby's dream of appointing a successor from within the club. After returning as caretaker-manager for six months, Busby then helped in the decision to appoint Frank O'Farrell, but he also struggled to pull the club back to winning ways. It was a time of massive readjustment, as several world-class players, including Charlton, Crerand and Law, were all nearing retirement.

Opposite: **Matt Busby and Alex Ferguson (left) pose with the European Cup Winners' Cup, which was won in dramatic style in May 1991, for the first time in the club's history, when United beat Barcelona.**

Added to that, Best's premature departure, during O'Farrell's reign, was a terrible loss to the club.

At the end of 1972 Tommy Docherty took over the reins, and his enthusiasm eventually rejuvenated the club. United were relegated at the end of the 1973-74 season, but they bounced straight back, winning the Second Division Championship in style with a superb young side. Once again, what saw United through a difficult period was the commitment of the fans. Average gates at Old Trafford during the season in the Second Division were 48,400, the highest in that division for 25 years. The fans deserve a lot of credit for helping to prevent the club from spiralling down. Although United are too big a club to have failed continuously, the history of the game is littered with the examples of big clubs, such as Newcastle and Wolves, who have struggled to halt a slide.

Back in the top flight, players such as Lou Macari, Steve Coppell, Martin Buchan, Stuart Pearson and Gordon Hill had the whole place buzzing again. Paul Ince, Lee Martin and Brian McClair are three among thousands of people who grew up admiring United during this period. After losing the FA Cup Final in 1976 to Southampton, in a season in which they had finished third, United won the FA Cup in 1977, beating champions Liverpool 2-1. United scored 103 goals during that pulsating season. I played for West Brom against Docherty's team in March 1977, in a 2-2 draw at Old Trafford in which Coppell and Hill scored. United were certainly an impressive, attacking side and the atmosphere of the 51,000 fans that day was memorable. These flying wingers were indicative of Tommy Docherty's fine transfer policy. Steve Coppell, who I later teamed up with at Manchester United, was one of the best buys the club has ever made.

After Docherty's departure in the summer of 1977, Dave Sexton arrived. When I played for the England Under-21 team in the late 1970s, they were managed by Sexton, and his understanding of the game was very impressive. In September 1980, when I was at West Brom, he offered £1 million to bring me to Old Trafford, but Ron Atkinson told him that he was not listening to offers for me.

It would have been interesting playing for Dave, because he certainly has the respect of players. He gets teams playing the way I feel they should play — passing the ball from your defence through the back, through midfield and to the feet of strikers. He knew that if club managers instill that in players, it helps the national team, because to have any real success at international level that is the way you have to play.

As manager of Manchester United, though, Sexton found the PR side of the manager's job difficult to handle. Although he built a solid team, for many fans it suffered in comparison to the exciting one that his predecessor had put together. But I don't think that Docherty's team would necessarily have been able to win the League Championship. Sexton tried to build some consistency into the team, because he thought the most important factor was to create a side that gave nothing away at the back.

In 1979 United reached the FA Cup Final, losing 3-2 to Arsenal in an encounter remembered for the dramatic last five minutes. A season later Sexton led

Guiding team-mates is a vital part of the captain's job on the field. I have been fortunate to have played with Martin Buchan and Ray Wilkins — two skippers who taught me a lot about the art of captaincy.

United to runners-up spot, their best League position since finishing there in 1967-68. That was the high point for him. After another season with still no trophies to show, the United Board decided that it was time for a change. In sacking Sexton, the directors showed the high standards they demand from a manager. Ironically, a blend of Sexton's defensive organisation and Docherty's attacking flair would probably have been unstoppable.

The Board eventually turned to my boss at West Brom, Ron Atkinson, to take on the challenge of running United. Four months later, in October 1981, he persuaded the Board to pay West Brom £1.8 million to bring me to the Reds. Playing for Manchester United is the biggest challenge any professional footballer can accept. I wanted that test and I had faith in the manager.

Atkinson's flamboyant approach seemed to work wonders. Within two seasons the FA Cup was back at United for the first time since 1977. Two years later, in even more dramatic circumstances, I lifted that famous trophy again. The FA Cup has that magical glory, but to a footballer the real proof of success is winning the championship — and that was Ron's overriding aim. United came mighty close to achieving that ambition in the 1985-86 season, when we began with 10 consecutive League victories at the start of the season, but injuries and other distractions broke our consistency and United's challenge evaporated. The absence of that trophy ultimately cost Atkinson his favourite job.

A new era at United started on 7th November 1986, the day Alex Ferguson arrived from Aberdeen to take over as our new boss. The players had been sad to see Ron leave, but it was possibly time for a change. As far as all the players, officials and our new boss were concerned the aim was and is still the same. The League Championship is the goal we are all aiming for at Old Trafford. Alex Ferguson left us in no doubt that it was his number one priority when he joined and over five years in the job has done nothing to diminish his appetite for that prize.

A glorious European night

We had a long hard struggle to get things right during his first few years at the club. Although his work did not bear immediate fruit, the manager had been rebuilding United from the foundations. He realised that the club had been surviving on its reputation for too long and needed major surgery. He set in motion a long-term strategy for success, with a key element of reviving the youth system at the club. During these momentous changes, however, we were plagued by bad luck and a string of appalling injuries — five United players had to retire from the game in the 1980s, and hundreds of weeks were spent on the treatment table by key players. We came in for some savage condemnation, but the players and directors were not too downcast, because we knew that the Boss was laying the foundations for success. Three major trophies in three seasons is proof of the first-rate work that was undertaken.

United started to show true character and commitment in the gritty FA Cup run of 1990, and in lifting the trophy we answered our critics in the best possible fashion. When I raised that Cup for the third time as United's captain, a record I am proud to hold, what gave me most pleasure about that win was that everyone, especially the fans, had been rewarded for sticking at it. Beating Steve Coppell's Crystal Palace, for United's seventh FA Cup win, was the reward that our hard graft had merited. The problem for a powerful club like Manchester United is that success is like food — the club cannot survive for long without it.

There is something about United that inspires jealousy and during that testing time Alex Ferguson had faced some vicious criticism. That victory certainly silenced our green-eyed censors and it has proved to be a turning point in the club's history. Confidence is the critical element of success in sport; ability on its own is not enough. To be victorious a team needs self-belief and that win proved, not least to ourselves, that we had the makings of a fine side. A year later, in a magical night in Rotterdam, we captured the European Cup Winners' Cup, beating Johan Cruyff's Barcelona, adding another glorious night to the club's list of landmarks.

Everyone at the club had been convinced that our European triumph would be the launching pad for a successful League challenge. We were all heartsick at throwing away the title right at the finishing post in the 1991-92 season. Although we were bitterly disappointed at finishing as runners-up, we know that we have to stay in the right frame of mind to complete the job, and that requires determination and faith. The players have it in their own capabilities, and Alex Ferguson has it in his ability as a manager. Soon after United's eighth postwar manager arrived from Aberdeen, Sir Matt Busby said: 'Alex has the ability to create a championship team — of that I am sure. It won't be easy and it won't happen overnight, because it's a difficult job. It might take a few seasons to get the players he wants and blend them into the side he wants.'

I believed when I first joined the club that I would go on to lift the championship as Manchester United's captain — and this ambition has burned in me for more than 11 years. But, as pundits never tire of reminding us, the last time United kicked off a title-winning season was on 20th August 1966. Although this is a record everyone at the club is desperate to break, it sometimes strikes me as funny that people keep reminding current players about that record. Some of my team-mates have been at the club for just a couple of years, and many colleagues, including Paul Ince, Lee Sharpe, Ryan Giggs and Andrei Kanchelskis, had not even been *born* when Charlton, Best and Law were parading the championship trophy around Old Trafford in 1967. The current United team should be judged on its own record, and the three cups won in three seasons, and the convincing challenge we put up for the title in 1991-92, should leave no one in any doubt that we are very close to achieving this ambition.

Playing with the greatest

It has been a long and disappointing wait for our supporters, but people sometimes forget that it took Busby seven years to secure his first title — and he went eight years between his third and fourth championship. All United's players since 1967 have wanted to be the first to break that title jinx, but some squads simply did not have the class to achieve that objective. The squad for the 1992-93 season is the finest for a quarter of a century, and the likes of myself, Brian McClair, Steve Bruce, Paul Ince, Gary Pallister, Ryan Giggs and Peter Schmeichel know that we will become legends ourselves when we win the League title.

Even though a championship medal has so far proved elusive, it has been an honour and a pleasure to play for Manchester United for over a decade — and under two of the best managers in the game. Those years have been some of the most tumultuous and testing in the club's 115-year history, but there has been no shortage of excitement or drama. During my career at the greatest club I have had the privilege of playing with some of the finest players in the history of the game. The following chapters are a record of my memorable times at Old Trafford.

BIG RON'S REIGN

On 6th June 1981 I played in England's 3-1 defeat of Hungary in a World Cup qualifier. A week earlier, we'd lost 2-1 to Switzerland in another World Cup match, so most of my thoughts at that time were taken up with these matches and I had not followed events at home too closely. During the flight home from Budapest a reporter told me that Ron Atkinson was definitely going to take over at Old Trafford.

Manchester United had considered a number of candidates to replace Dave Sexton, including Lawrie McMenemy, Ron Saunders, Bobby Robson and Billy McNeill. In the end they turned to Atkinson, who officially became manager on 9th June 1981, on

Ron Atkinson (*below*) and myself in action for United.

a three-year contract. He has the sort of personality that will galvanise any football club in the world, even one as big as United, and he strengthened his hand by replacing Sexton's backroom staff — Tommy Cavanagh, Harry Gregg, Jack Crompton and Laurie Brown — with Mick Brown and Brian Whitehouse, who had also left the Hawthorns.

Sexton's team had finished as runners-up in 1979-80, but in the season before Atkinson's arrival they had finished eighth, 12 points behind champions Aston Villa. United had gone out of both cup competitions in early rounds for the past two seasons. Ron decided that the team had to be totally rebuilt. Heading the list of players he wanted were Glenn Hoddle and Frank Stapleton, the latter to replace Joe Jordan, who had left in July for A.C. Milan. After two months at the club Atkinson had announced that he wanted to sign me, and he made an official offer at the start of September.

'Pay every penny for Robson!'

Atkinson's departure from the Hawthorns had been disappointing for me personally. West Brom should have allowed him to spend more money. We had a good squad, but it needed improving. The club had allowed class players, such as Laurie Cunningham, to leave; when they let the manager go as well, that made my mind up: I wanted to go to a big club who were determined to win things. West Brom were going about it the wrong way, and I think their record in the 1980s shows my fears were justified. They had seven different managers that decade, and at the end of the 1990-91 season were relegated to the Third Division for the first time in their history.

I did not, initially at least, have my heart set on going to Manchester United. Arsenal had sounded me out in 1980 — at about the same time that Sexton had tried to sign me for United — and Liverpool were considering making an offer. Given the interest from Anfield, it is ironic that when Ron Atkinson had discussed my transfer with Bill Shankly, the former Liverpool boss had actually urged him to sign me for United. 'Ron,' he said. 'Pay every penny it takes to get Robson, every penny!'

If I am totally honest, I must admit that both clubs appealed to me, but Liverpool were not able to spare the money at that time — for a fee that broke the British record. However, once I knew for sure that Manchester United were definitely bidding for me, then I set my heart on playing for them. The appeal of performing in front of so many supporters swayed my decision, as did the challenge of having to win something every year to satisfy the club's tremendous ambitions. Eleven seasons later I can still get excited by these two things.

I have always felt thankful to Ron. He put his head on the chopping block by persuading the Board to invest such a lot of money in me. Since arriving I have talked to numerous friends in Manchester about this, and they have told me that at that time a lot of people were saying: 'Who is this Bryan Robson that United have broken the bank to buy?'

There were problems with the move that had to be ironed out. West Brom's Chairman, Bert Millichip, said: 'Robson is one player who is not available at any price', and Ron's successor, Ronnie Allen, said that I would leave over his dead body. West Brom had offered me a six-year contract, but I was adamant that I wanted to leave. When West Brom were knocked out of the UEFA Cup by Zurich Grasshoppers, the Board's opposition weakened.

Below: **Frank Stapleton, number 9, thumps the ball past his former Arsenal team-mate Pat Jennings, during our 4-2 League Cup semi-final win in 1983.**

At the same time, Remi Moses had gone to see Ron Atkinson to ask for a move. He was a Moss Side lad, and while we were at West Brom he always used to come back to Manchester after a game. I had no idea that Remi would be involved in the deal, but he was out of contract and both clubs agreed on a fee.

The pressure disturbs me

The day I joined Manchester United was one of the most exciting of my life. On Saturday 3rd October 1981 I signed in front of 46,837 witnesses at Old Trafford before watching my new team-mates thrash Wolves 5-0. It had been a tremendous thrill to hear United's supporters chant my name. It was an easy move. I was on good terms with Ron, and his assistant Mick Brown, and knew how they wanted me to fit into the team. I was familiar with Steve Coppell and Ray Wilkins from the England scene, and many of the established stars went out of their way to help me settle in. The club itself appeared to have more of a family atmosphere than Albion. There was a buoyant mood when I started. The players were enjoying the new practice sessions, and instead of disappearing after training, the players went to the canteen for something to eat. This seemed to generate a healthy team spirit.

United's victory against Wolves was the ninth League game of the season, and our fourth win. My debut came in a League Cup match at Spurs, which we lost 1-0. Although it would not rank as one of my finest performances, I was happy enough just to have come through it. My League debut came in a

Above: **Liverpool's Bruce Grobbelaar takes his 'keeper as sweeper' role a bit too far, as he rushes out during the 1983 Milk Cup Final and brings down Gordon McQueen, who was heading for goal.**

passionate Manchester derby, which ended scoreless. After that game we finally started to pick up form and achieved a sweet victory against the eventual champions Liverpool. Whenever I'd been to Anfield with West Brom we always seemed to lose about 4-0. If we came away with a two-goal defeat we counted it a breakthrough, but the moment the match was mentioned, our players were confident they would win. At the time, United were probably the only side in Britain who went there with this attitude.

I thoroughly enjoyed that day. I made a few strong runs forward and it was my free kick that led to Kevin Moran's goal. Although Liverpool equalised from the penalty spot, we went straight back on to the attack and scored a last-gasp winner through Arthur Albiston, who played a great one-two with Frank Stapleton before coolly placing his shot beyond a young Bruce Grobbelaar.

This was followed by victory at Sunderland, where I grabbed my first goal for United. I always enjoy playing in the northeast — the supporters there are fantastically loyal and passionate — and winning 5-1 at Roker Park was very pleasing. It meant I could face going out and having a pint with my dad after the game. I am not sure that would have been advisable if the score had been the other way around, because he still has more than a touch of black-and-white Newcastle blood running through his veins.

A run of wins — in the first season after the introduction of three points for a win — established

United as leaders. I had been reasonably content with my play up until then, but I subsequently went through about two months when I had a really bad time. I was so keyed up to prove that United had been right to buy me, that it affected my play. In the end I forced myself to relax, to ignore the tag of being Britain's most expensive player and got on with enjoying my football. I must have done something right, because at the end of the season I was chosen in a midfield position in the PFA First Division side.

As my own form had improved the team had gone into a lull, and the second half of the season was an anticlimax. On 2nd January we went out of the FA Cup in the third round, losing 1-0 at Watford. Our confidence took a bit of a knock and we won only six of the next 15 League games. The boss picked us up and we won seven of our last nine games to finish third, five points behind Ipswich Town and nine points behind champions Liverpool. Ironically, this would turn out to be the highest League position achieved under Atkinson in five seasons at the club.

Atkinson had felt the tension at first and it had been a season of experimentation. He had spent a lot of money on new players. John Gidman had a steady season at right-back, Frank Stapleton finished as United's top scorer, I had found my feet and although Remi had missed 22 games that year all Ron's signings had won over the crowd. There had

been some encouraging developments in the season. Norman Whiteside, a prodigiously talented teenager, had broken into the first team; and Paul McGrath had been bought for a bargain £25,000.

Some of my colleagues had been in a state of limbo at the start of Ron's reign, because they had not then won the Boss's vote of confidence, but he decided that Gary Bailey, Mike Duxbury, Kevin Moran and Arthur Albiston, were part of his plans for the future — although Sammy McIlroy, Jimmy Nicholl, Garry Birtles, Mickey Thomas and Paddy Roche were not.

There was an air of great expectancy as we approached the 1982-83 season. In the close season Atkinson had signed Arnold Muhren from Ipswich on a free transfer. He gave us tremendous balance on the left side of midfield and we started well in the League, winning five of our opening six matches, but we faded badly in October, winning only one game. Our confidence had been badly bruised by an early exit in the UEFA Cup. We had drawn 0-0 at home to Valencia, but lost 2-1 in Spain. United had been without Muhren in both legs. Arnold had won a UEFA Cup winners' medal with Ipswich in 1981 and his experience would have been invaluable.

United started the Milk Cup campaign against Bournemouth. In the first leg, which we won 2-0 at home, Peter Beardsley made his only first-team appearance for United, and in the second leg, Ray

Wilkins broke his cheek bone. At the time of his injury, Ray was captain of Manchester United and England. I replaced him in both jobs. We then disposed of Bradford City and Southampton, and knocked out Brian Clough's Nottingham Forest in a superb 4-0 quarter-final win at Old Trafford, earning a place against Arsenal in the semi-final.

Our League form had been inconsistent, however, and we knew that any success would have to come in a cup competition. Although facing the Gunners is always a daunting task, on a frozen Highbury pitch, in the first leg, United gave a devastating display of power and artistry and hammered Arsenal 4-2. Our display included some of the best football of any United team I have played in. Muhren picked out Stapleton time after time with accurate, dangerous through balls, and Coppell, who scored twice, tore the Arsenal defence to pieces, which was no mean feat considering he was being marked by Kenny Sansom. Steve ran riot that night. To go down to Arsenal and be 4-0 up in a cup semi-final was a hell of a performance. United had a daft last 10 minutes, when we conceded two soft goals, but we had annihilated them overall. We won the second leg 2-1, but I damaged my ankle ligaments and that injury kept me out for nearly two months.

In that time, United made further progress in the FA Cup, beating West Ham, Luton and Derby before overcoming Everton in the quarter-final. Sadly, my battle for fitness failed and I missed playing in United's first League Cup Final. The lads were on top of their game, having lost only one out of the previous 17 games. Norman Whiteside scored a brilliant opening goal against Liverpool after 12 minutes. Gordon McQueen floated a pass from the halfway line to Whiteside, who was being shadowed by Alan Hansen, on the edge of the box. Norman left him for dead with one turn, taking the ball on the inside with his left foot and then running on to it and placing a low shot home with his right foot.

One of my all-time great games

This was a frustrating game to watch from the sidelines, because a series of freak events turned the tie in Liverpool's favour. First, Alan Kennedy's shot bounced in front of Gary Bailey before going in. Then, Gordon McQueen and Kevin Moran were injured during the game and we had to play extra time with Lou Macari at full-back and Frank Stapleton at centre-half. But for those injuries we definitely would have held our lead and won the Cup.

On 9th April I scored in my comeback game against Southampton. A week later, on a sunny day at Villa Park, we beat Arsenal in a scintillating FA Cup semi-final that I still look back on as one of the most enjoyable matches of my career. United were without Coppell and Muhren, and Arsenal, led by Don Howe and Terry Neill, were an experienced cup team. By the 37th minute, we were trailing to a Tony Woodcock goal. Our season could have ended in massive disappointment on that field. Arsenal had a host of impressive players — including Kenny Sansom, John Hollins, David O'Leary and Graham Rix — and they were convinced they would hold out.

I always enjoyed playing with Ray Wilkins. *Left:* **Here, Ray nicks the ball away from our opponent to set another attack in motion. I have played with Ray at all levels from youth international to full England matches — he won 84 full caps — and I rate him as one of the finest midfield players of the past 20 years. Ray, who was bought for £825,000 by Dave Sexton in August 1979, picked up an unfair reputation for being a negative player, but his team-mates at United were always impressed by his skill and ability to execute a telling through ball. He could also strike the ball well, and in the FA Cup Final against Brighton he scored our second goal, in a 2-2 draw, with a beautiful long-range curler. We were all determined to do well in the replay and my two goals helped us run out as 4-0 winners — the biggest winning margin in a Wembley final.**

We proved we were fighters

Nobody could have doubted our talent, but that day we proved we were a team of fighters. To come back from a goal down in an FA Cup semi-final and win 2-1 took a lot of bottle. I was delighted to score our equaliser. It made me feel that I had really started to repay the faith everyone had shown in me. I got on the end of a pass and held off Brian Talbot to shoot past George Wood. Then Norman Whiteside scored the winner with a superb shot. He ran on to Arthur Albiston's pass and hit a cracking first-time volley, his 12th goal of the season. I was jubilant at the end and in my joy gave my shirt away to a fan as I ran off, relinquishing a prize memento.

There had been real doubt about who would make the starting line-up for the FA Cup Final. Moses had definitely been ruled out by suspension after he had been sent off in a bad-tempered League match with Arsenal. In late March United had acquired Laurie Cunningham on loan from Real Madrid and Ron Atkinson had pencilled him in to replace Steve Coppell, who had a knee injury, but Cunningham unselfishly declared himself unfit. The boss chose the late Welsh Under-21 international Alan Davies.

United were regarded as racing certainties for the final. Brighton had finished bottom of the First Division, but they had beaten Liverpool 2-1 at Anfield on the road to Wembley. Gordon Smith put the Seagulls ahead early on, but we pulled ourselves together in the second half. Stapleton equalised and then Wilkins scored a brilliant goal, curling a long range shot into the top corner. Gary Stevens made it all square and right at the end of extra time, Smith squandered a golden chance for Brighton. We all agreed that we had been let off the hook.

Scoring in an FA Cup Final

United had been well below par in the first game, and although we were unchanged in team for the replay, United were different in attitude, determined to get a complete grip on the game. The replay was on a Thursday evening, without the tension of a day of TV coverage, and this seemed to help us. Two goals in a four-minute spell in the first half put the game beyond Brighton. Alan Davies set up our first, crossing for me to drive home. What a brilliant feeling to score a goal in a Cup Final. Just after that, Davies touched on Muhren's corner for Whiteside to score our second, and he thus became the first player to score in a League Cup and FA Cup Final in the same season. Just before the break I added our third.

The atmosphere in the dressing room was pretty buoyant at half-time, but we were in no mood for complacency. In the second half we increased our lead with an Arnold Muhren penalty, giving United the biggest winning margin in a Wembley FA Cup Final. The champagne certainly flowed that evening, which was Matt Busby's 74th birthday. Later, when the players reflected on the season, we agreed that with more strength in defence — we conceded 51 goals in all, scoring 92 (15 of which I had bagged) — we would have been capable of challenging for the title. Nevertheless, it had been a satisfying season and we had played some great football.

United began the 1983-84 pre-season warm-up with some unusual games — in Swaziland! The success of the previous season had persuaded Ron Atkinson to continue with the same squad, and only Ashley Grimes and Martin Buchan, who had spent 10 years at the club, had left. The sole new face was Arthur Graham, bought from Leeds United for £65,000. Sadly, after battling with a serious knee injury for two years, Steve Coppell was forced to retire at the age of 28. That was a calamity not only for United but for England.

The season started on a high note when we beat Liverpool 2-0 at Wembley in the Charity Shield. This was their first year under Joe Fagan, following Bob Paisley's retirement, and they were keen to

Opposite: **Another happy memory from 1983 as I raise the FA Charity Shield after Manchester United had beaten Joe Fagan's Liverpool 2-0. I scored both goals in our victory that day.**

impress, but we played well that day and I netted both goals. We opened our League campaign by winning four out of our first five games.

Much of our effort that season was reserved for the Cup Winners' Cup. In the first round we drew 1-1 at home with Dukla Prague, and fought back in the away leg to earn a 2-2 draw, with goals from Stapleton and myself, winning through on the away goals rule. Our manager rated it as one of the finest games he had ever seen. In the next round United had a more comfortable passage against Spartak Varna, beating them 4-1 on aggregate, and once again I got on the scoresheet.

Good cheer in Europe was followed by gloom at home when we were knocked out of the League Cup by Oxford United, in a second replay, and went out at Bournemouth in our first game as FA Cup holders. To be knocked out of the two domestic cups by Third Division clubs, after reaching the finals of both competitions the previous year, just goes to show what a daft game football can be.

The crowd had the pitch shaking

United had not been able to force the pace in the League despite an unbeaten run from 4th December until 31st March, because we had drawn seven of the 16 games played in that period, which made us even more determined to do well in the quarter-final of the Cup Winners' Cup against Barcelona. Our first leg 2-0 defeat was a travesty of justice.

Before the second leg, the manager was at his best, relaxed and expansive. Atkinson told us to forget the first leg and treat it as a one-off tie. The whole team was sensational, producing one of the most glorious games in the club's history. Barcelona had Diego Maradona and were fancied strongly, but he did not perform at all that evening, thankfully. When Whiteside hit the crossbar early on, it did not dishearten us, but drove us on like men possessed. After winning a corner I decided to take up a position at the far post. Graeme Hogg flicked on Ray Wilkins's corner and I flew in among the boots to score with a diving header. A deafening cheer erupted. It was the best atmosphere I have ever witnessed at Old Trafford. The crowd of 58,547 had the pitch shaking.

We charged on for the second half knowing that we were 1-0 up and playing towards the Stretford End. It seemed as if 15,000 people were sucking the ball into the net. Shortly after the interval Barcelona were passing the ball between defenders, but when Victor rolled it back to their goalkeeper, big Norman was on him like a greyhound. The ball broke loose, Moses hared after it and sent over a cross which was met on the volley by Wilkins. The 'keeper could only parry the shot and I thumped the ball home.

Minutes later I found Arthur Albiston with a crossfield ball, and his centre was headed back across the goal by Whiteside. Stapleton, on the edge of the six-yard box, hammered the ball into the roof of the net. After United's third goal the Spaniards came back into the game, and we had put so much into the

first 75 minutes that we were out on our feet. The euphoria of the supporters gave us the will to keep going and at the final whistle, fans flooded on to the pitch to carry me off on their shoulders. Bobby Charlton, who smiled like a Cheshire cat that night, said: 'The immense joy resulting from that victory surpassed *anything* I have ever experienced in the game. It was even better than winning the FA Cup.' People were moved by the sheer bottle of that team. To win 3-0 would have been a splendid achievement in itself, but we had done it playing stylish football.

'Moses obliterated Platini'

That set up a semi-final against Juventus. Ron Atkinson described, in an interview for this book, the circumstances of the game: 'Juventus had about nine members of the Italian squad that had won the World Cup in 1982. In the first leg we were without Muhren, who was injured, and Wilkins, who was suspended. A day before the match I was being interviewed at our training ground by some Italian journalists. As the players were finishing a practice session, I glanced out of my office window. I watched Robbo pass a few footballs back to be collected and as he kicked one, I saw him pull up and seize the back of his leg. That hamstring injury put him out of the match. It could not have come at a worse time.

We were leading the First Division and about to go into the most important European encounter for 16 years. We had been playing a new system without orthodox wide men, using Robbo as a sort of deep lying third striker behind Stapleton and Whiteside.

'That left us facing a really hard task against Juventus, but we gave it a bloody good go. Moses was superb. He was in a makeshift midfield with John Gidman, Arthur Graham, Paul McGrath and Alan Davies. Alan had broken his ankle in a pre-season friendly and it was his first senior game since the Cup Final replay. Moses, United's playmaker, obliterated Michel Platini. Davies scored in a 1-1 draw. We knew it would be tough to get a result in Italy but we played well there and were level 1-1 until the final minute, when we were beaten by a classic Paolo Rossi suckerpunch. Their boss, Giovanni Trapattoni, admitted they had been on the rocks. That was our best chance of winning the trophy.'

With 10 games remaining in the League, United had been ahead of Liverpool, but there was a sudden loss of form, coupled to our injury crisis, and we claimed only 10 points out of 30. United, who had spent much of the season in a two-horse race for title, finished fourth. I had really enjoyed playing in

Below: **Alan Davies, making his first senior appearance since the 1983 FA Cup Final replay, slots home our equaliser in the 1-1 draw with Juventus in the first leg of the Cup Winners' semi-final in 1984.**

that advanced role and I scored 18 goals that season, my best total ever. I had attracted the attention of Italian scouts. That put doubts in my mind about the future, and what would be best for my family, but at least the speculation did not affect my performances.

Throughout the last third of the season, barely a day had passed without my being asked whether I would be leaving United. Ron Atkinson's response had been to price me at over £3 million and that proved a sufficiently large sum to deter potential buyers. A.C. Milan, Sampdoria and Juventus were definitely interested in buying me at the time.

I would have done well in Italy

If I had left Manchester United I would probably have headed for Juventus, because they offered so many world-class team-mates, including Rossi, Boniek, Platini, Scirea and Tardelli. Juventus was the place to go to win medals; they proved that by winning the Italian League and the Cup Winners' Cup in 1984, and the European Cup in 1985. Michel Platini was the one player that I really wanted to team up with, and that prospect made a move to Italy very inviting. It would have been impossible to turn down if Juventus had put the money up front and if United had accepted their bid. Under those circumstances I would not have refused that move, because if it had come off it would have meant the chance to realise so many ambitions. But Ron knew that putting such a high price tag on me would probably drive them away. I know that some players, even first-rate ones such as Ian Rush, have struggled to fit in abroad, but I think there is a gap for players like myself in the Italian League — something David Platt has demonstrated in his career in Italy — and I believe I would have done well there if I had gone.

In the event, it was Ray Wilkins who went to Italy, signing for A.C. Milan for £1.5 million. It was disappointing to lose a top-class player, but I was not jealous. I was pleased when he made a success of his career in Italy. The departure of Wilkins did leave a big hole at United, as Steve Coppell said: 'It is my belief that if Ray had stayed in that 1984-85 season, and played with some of the new signings, United would have cleaned up.'

Prompted by the disappointment of ending such a promising season with no trophies, and having the money from the Wilkins sale to play with, Ron Atkinson made a host of big signings that summer. Gordon Strachan, Alan Brazil and Jesper Olsen arrived at the club, along with my old West Brom colleague Peter Barnes. Of my 10 team-mates who started the 1984-85 season, only four — Bailey, Albiston, Moses and Moran — had been with me on my League debut three years before.

We drew our first four games, but when we beat Newcastle United 5-0 at Old Trafford early in September, we started to show our real quality. Newcastle had Peter Beardsley, Chris Waddle, David McCreery and Glenn Roeder in their team that day, but they were simply brushed aside by a brilliant performance from the Reds. There were lovely flowing moves and superb goals. Our new wingers were dribbling with panache, our passing was swift, and accompanied by terrific movement off the ball. Moses capped a fine one-touch first time passing move between four players with a splendid finish.

In October 1984 I ended the speculation about my career by signing a new seven-year contract. Martin Edwards said it was the biggest and longest ever offered to a Manchester United player. I had talked the whole matter through with my wife, Denise, and we had decided that the best policy was to secure our future in England. There have been two major decisions in my playing career — the other was leaving West Brom. I knew that committing myself to United would not be a gamble. My family was happy living in Manchester, and I thought Atkinson's new team was capable of great things.

Alan Brazil bagged five goals in October and the team scored freely throughout the first four months of the season, but we were short of being a consistently good team. Our League campaign began to stutter and United's UEFA Cup quest ended in the quarter-final when we lost 5-4 on penalties, after extra time, to Videoton. That defeat made us even more determined to capture the FA Cup. En route to face Liverpool in the semi-final, we had knocked out Bournemouth, Coventry, Blackburn and West Ham. Liverpool were the favourites, even though we had won 1-0 at Anfield, with a superb header from Frank Stapleton, in the League encounter just two weeks before, but United came through after two classic confrontations.

Kevin's sending off was a joke

To win the FA Cup we had to beat Everton. Howard Kendall's team had beaten us 5-0 in the League and dumped us out of the League Cup. They had won the championship, setting a new record of 90 points, had captured the Cup Winners' Cup and were going for the treble. Both defences were on top in the Final, but everyone thought the odds were in Everton's favour, especially when we went down to 10 men with about 12 minutes left. Kevin Moran had become the first player to be sent off in an FA Cup Final. His dismissal was a joke decision and it incensed our players. If Kevin's challenge had been even a split second earlier he would have got the ball cleanly, and Peter Reid (an honest pro), the man he tackled, accepted that the tackle was not malicious.

Five minutes into extra time, Mark Hughes made room for himself in midfield and swung a brilliant, lethargic-looking pass out to Whiteside on the wing. The Everton defenders scurried back into the box, while Gordon Strachan made a run on the overlap and screamed for the ball. Norman, who was covered by a defender, moved in from the far right, shuffled his feet and, without warning, let fly a curling shot that bent as accurately as a guided missile into the net, past the despairing lunge of Neville Southall. Norman's goal is one of the best there has ever been in an FA Cup Final. He took on a defender in a wide position, was still aware of which part of the goal to aim at and executed the shot with phenomenal skill. There was nothing flukey about it. Norman used to do that in training all the time, coming in from the wing and bending the ball into the net. It is one thing to accomplish it in a practice game, but it takes ice-cool nerve to do it in front of 100,000 fans at Wembley.

United had lost only three games in the second half of the season and that Cup win gave us an extra lift of confidence. Hughes had scored 17 League goals, the best individual scoring performance at United for 13 years, and the team had netted 113 goals in 60 games, the highest total ever scored in a season by United. Our Boss felt more confident. He had grown to live with the pressures of the job and players found him much more approachable.

By the time I returned for pre-season training from a busy schedule with England — playing Romania, Finland and Scotland before going to Mexico City to play Italy and West Germany — I was bang on form and the team were really confident. We won our first 10 League games, conceding only three goals, and looked set to break Spurs' 25-year record of 11 consecutive First Division victories. Matt Busby, who was celebrating 40 years at Old Trafford, said: 'It is all coming together now. You could say we're United again! Ron and his staff have done a first class job of bringing together so many individuals, who are my kinds of players, and turned them into a team who play my kind of football. You have to hand it to Ron. He knew exactly what he wanted and has done it his own way. This team excites me.'

An injury curse hits United

We didn't even equal Spurs' record, however: we drew our 11th game at Luton. Hughes gave us the lead, but Brian Stein scored the equaliser. Things were never the same after that game. I tore my hamstring playing for England, the worst hamstring injury I have ever suffered, and it seemed as if there was a curse on us. John Gidman broke his leg and Gordon Strachan, who'd been playing exceptionally well, dislocated his shoulder. Even though he was back after six weeks, he did not adapt to the physical side of the game for a long while after that injury.

The worst part of being a footballer is when you are forced to sit on the sidelines and watch the team lose. It is easy to relax when the team is picking up points, but when things go wrong it is intensely frustrating, because it is impossible to stop thinking that you would be able to help the team if you were out on the pitch. It really plays on your mind. Unfortunately, this was something I had to go through again at the end of the 1991-92 season, and that time proved to be even more dispiriting.

After returning against Sheffield Wednesday I twisted my ankle, which put me out for a further 10 games. In that time we were knocked out of the League Cup by Liverpool and lost League games to Arsenal, Everton and Nottingham Forest. I was certainly unlucky with injuries — and none more so than when I fell awkwardly in the game at West Ham,

dislocating again the shoulder I had first damaged the previous season. There were amateur experts on every paper telling me what to do about the dislocated shoulder, but after consulting a specialist, there was only one realistic decision. Six weeks from the time of the dislocation, England were due to start the preparation for the World Cup, and the Finals would start about a month after that. An operation on the shoulder would have sidelined me for at least three months. Not only would that have put me out of the World Cup, it would have meant missing the crucial run-in to United's League campaign.

It is downhill if you leave United

People were urging me to have an operation, but I chose the alternative course of action, which was to try and build up the muscle in the shoulder and play on, even through some pain. I even tried playing in a harness that a rugby player from New Zealand had sent to me. The harness was probably great for playing rugby, because you could run freely with it on, but it affected my balance. Every time I went to head or lined myself up for a shot or pass the harness pulled me down, so I had to abandon using it.

At the same time as I was battling with my shoulder injury, Hughes went off the boil for United. He had signed a five-year contract at the start of the season, but in January 1986, when United were playing at Oxford, the news broke that he would be a Barcelona player by June. Mark had scored 10 goals in our first 15 games, but after that game at the Manor Ground, he scored once in 17 games. Mark later admitted: 'In that final six months at United before heading off to Spain I was living a nightmare. I hardly spent an evening without hitting a bar somewhere in town. Burning a hole in me was the fact that basically I didn't want to leave.'

In the end, Liverpool took the title and Manchester United finished fourth, 12 points behind them. I had made only 21 appearances. Players never like to make injuries an excuse for failure, but to a man we were convinced that if we had stayed free of injuries there was not a team in the land who would have caught us. It had been a thoroughly disheartening end to the season, and worse was to come for me personally in the summer. The hardest part of a World Cup campaign is qualifying, and I was looking forward to playing in Mexico. My shoulder held up in England's opening game against Portugal, but it went during the game against Morocco. Bobby Robson was kind enough to say later: 'Bryan is the complete player. I am sure that with a fully fit Robson, England would have won the World Cup in 1986.' It was probably worse in Italy in 1990, when I injured my achilles tendon and had to come home early from a World Cup Finals again, because at least when I had gone to Mexico I had known there was a risk of that happening.

During that summer Ron Atkinson had done a lot of soul-searching, and although he later told me that his instincts told him to quit, he decided to stay on and try to win that elusive title. The thing that brings you to Manchester United is ambition, and if you have any in you, which Ron certainly does, then Old Trafford is the place to be. It doesn't matter how much success our rivals have had, United are the biggest club in the land. If you leave United you go downhill. That is what finally persuaded Ron to stay, even though he had received lucrative offers from other clubs. He thought that he could rebuild the team, but he was not under any illusions about the task he faced: 'I always knew it could be sudden-death for me in 1986,' he said.

Ron had opponents on the Board who had misgivings about his spending policy, and that hampered his room for manoeuvre. He thought that United were sometimes 'naive at the back' and

needed a centre-half to partner Paul McGrath, but he missed out on signing Terry Butcher. I had thought that Terry was definitely coming to the club and the fact that he did not was a big disappointment to Ron Atkinson. Terry was a proven international, but he was allowed to go to Glasgow Rangers. At the time, Terry himself told me that he would love to come to Manchester United. That episode indicated that the writing was on the wall for Atkinson.

At the start of the season, United had been plagued by reports of ill-discipline, but the amount of friction within the squad was exaggerated. I would not describe it as the most settled squad of all those I have been in at United, and a few altercations between players definitely did not help morale, but

THE TITLE THAT SLIPPED AWAY

successive League wins, and one victory in the League Cup, there were six splendid performances and five that were nothing special, but that run suddenly meant that we were within one game of setting a new Football League record of consecutive Division One wins at the start of a season.

Even though we drew our 11th League game and failed to break the record, I was confident that it was going to be our season. I still don't think that we would have been caught that year but for the injuries we picked up, and some of them were so unfortunate. Bryan Robson snapped his hamstring playing for England against Turkey, when he was chasing a lost ball. That put him out for weeks. He made a couple of abortive comebacks but was hit by that dreadful shoulder injury. Then there were a crop of injuries that autumn to Gordon Strachan, Graeme Hogg and Mick Duxbury and coming all at once it threw our rhythm totally out of joint.

Despite these setbacks, we made a valiant attempt to pick ourselves up, but we were never able to sustain a revival, and it fell apart completely in two games near the start of April. United lost 2-1 at home to Chelsea in a live game. We had totally battered them, but Kerry Dixon scored a last-gasp winner. That, followed by a home defeat against Sheffield Wednesday,

killed the season for us and we ended in fourth place, which was a joke really.

That was a painful season to recover from and it is very feasible that it would have been in my best interests to have left United that summer. There were a couple of clubs sounding me out and maybe, on reflection, that would have been the right decision, but I was still sure I could win things.

In that summer of 1986, a number of United players went out with the England, Scotland and Northern Ireland squads to the World Cup Finals in Mexico. Five of my players, including Robbo, had to have operations when they came back. It meant that right away we were up against it. I was concerned about some of our defensive frailties, and it has been well documented that I tried to sign Ipswich Town's Terry Butcher, who had proved himself such a fine player in the World Cup. After working hard to set up a deal I was refused permission to buy him.

Starting that 1986-87 season with a central defence pairing of Butcher and McGrath would have made all the difference. We would have been strong enough to have kept in contention for honours while key players recovered from injury. But that didn't happen and the Board gave me only two months, which was not sufficient time to turn the club around again.'

In an interview for this book, Ron Atkinson (above) *talked about the eventful 1985-86 season: 'We did play some great stuff at the start of that season, but not in all of the 10 games we won on the trot. It was unfortunate that there was a dispute about televised soccer at the time, and football was off the screens, so people did not necessarily get a balanced view of how things were going.*

There were some games in which we played terrific football — I can remember in particular a couple of thrilling high-scoring wins against Manchester City and Nottingham Forest — but the overall standard seems to have improved in the mind's eye as time has gone by. Indeed, there were a few matches where we scraped a victory. We opened the season by losing the Charity Shield against Everton and then, after an impressive 4-0 win against Aston Villa, we nicked a 1-0 win at Ipswich with a goal from Robbo. On balance, out of those 10

Above: Referee Peter Willis is deaf to all entreaties as he orders off Kevin Moran during the 1985 FA Cup Final. Moran became the first player ever to be dismissed in an FA Cup Final. *Right:* Kevin, second from the left, sits anxiously on the bench, following his sending off. *Below:* A moment of sheer ecstasy as Norman Whiteside's wonderful shot curls beyond the despairing lunge of Neville Southall to give United victory.

dressing room tiffs are not remarkable in football. At West Brom, there used to be bust-ups all the time that ended in head-to-head confrontations. Lads would get annoyed at each other and it would end in a fight, often nothing more than handbags at 10 paces. Those months at the start of the 1985-86 season were the only time I have seen that happen at United. Ron loved the camaraderie of the dressing room, and was close to some of the players, which made it all the harder for him to repair the situation.

Players make or break a boss

United's problems off the pitch would have passed unnoticed but for our poor form on the field. In November 1985 United had been riding high at the top of the table. A year later we had won three out of 13 League games and were four places from the bottom of the First Division. Atkinson said United would pull away from trouble, but he had lost the confidence of some of the players, as Frank Stapleton said: 'Atkinson did not seem able to give us that little something that would get us out of the rut, he seemed to think that because we had so much experience it would just happen.' The Board had been worried by falling gates — there had been 'only' 32,440 at Old Trafford for the 109th derby game in October, the lowest ever for a visit by Manchester City, and 20,000 down on the previous season.

After a 4-1 defeat at Southampton in the League Cup, the Board moved speedily. Atkinson said: 'I had no indication it was going to happen until I got the call to see the Chairman. I was just getting ready for a nice five-a-side game.' Players are never pleased when a manager gets the sack, because it is the results the players have produced that make or break a manager. It reflects on you as much as on him. All in all, though, it was probably best for everybody that the decision was taken. The team was heading down a cul-de-sac, out of which we didn't seem capable of finding our way.

'Be proud of this club' Ron said

Nevertheless, Ron Atkinson went proudly. He called the players together and said: 'Hold your heads up. Remember your pride and be proud of this club because it is the finest in the business.' He didn't whine, because that is not his style. On the night of his dismissal he asked a few friends round to his house for some drinks. Gordon Strachan and myself were invited. We spent the evening talking football with him — that is the kind of man he is. It had been a big blow to him, and it hurt, but he still invited people round, put on a jolly face and made sure we all had a good night.

Atkinson did not get the breaks he deserved in that last season. I am convinced that his flashy image helped cost him the job he loved most of all. The public just didn't take to him at Old Trafford. They thought he was a publicity-seeker and big-headed.

He does take pleasure in wearing well-cut suits and quality jewellery, but this image of a Champagne Charlie is misleading. I have known Ron for more than 15 years and it is a caricature of a hard-working, knowledgeable man. He does like a glass of bubbly, but more often than not he will buy the champagne and pour it in someone else's glass, while, if you watch closely, his glass stays at the same level. His image may have been a good thing for West Brom, bringing welcome publicity to a provincial club, but Manchester United has charisma enough already and some people resented his behaviour.

Ron was a great motivator. He relaxed the players before big games because he himself showed no nerves and just treated the preparation, even if it was a semi-final or a Wembley final, as if it was an ordinary game, which took all the heat out of the situation. It helped the players unwind, and the more relaxed players are, the better the performance is, because you are not burning up nervous energy by worrying. Under him, United lost only 12 Cup matches out of the 65 they played — winning in great attacking style, particularly in the high pressure games. He was superb at getting his message across and always stressed our own strengths and the value of positive thinking. There were a few players who did not have a great deal of time for his style of management, but any boss who is in charge of so many people will always rub some up the wrong way.

Atkinson's teams were stylish

Although his teams played 'off the cuff' football, United's attacking patterns were not random, they were practised and refined on the training ground. We would play head tennis, five-a-side games to hone our passing skills and close control, and the emphasis was always on enjoying training as much as possible. Ron loved joining in our sessions — I didn't mind him participating as long as he was not on my side!

During our marvellous run at the start of the 1985-86 season, Atkinson had said: 'For me the performance is as important as the result, and I firmly believe that if you put enough performances together you get the results.' He loved swagger and panache, and he could coax good performances from players. He gave youngsters a chance and was true to his philosophy at Old Trafford — he bought flair players and always encouraged us to attack. It is no coincidence that he went on to further success after leaving Old Trafford, transforming Atletico Madrid during his brief spell in Spain and leading Sheffield Wednesday to promotion from Division Two in 1991 and to a Rumbelows League Cup win in the same season — ironically at Manchester United's expense.

I will always have a special affection for Ron, because he brought me to Manchester United, and while he was at Old Trafford he built teams that were victorious and attractive to watch. Two FA Cup wins in five seasons is success by any standards. In sacking Ron Atkinson the Board showed that they will accept nothing less from a Manchester United manager than the League Championship.

ATKINSON'S ALLSTARS

Manchester United are one of the standard-bearers for British football and to satisfy the supporters the team must be successful — and stylish. A large section of the Reds' support had grown increasingly impatient with the style of football under Dave Sexton. United fans insist on entertaining football and Ron Atkinson addressed this demand at his first press conference at Old Trafford: 'I will not be just United's manager, I will be an ardent fan. If the team bores me, it will be boring our supporters, who hero-worship the players. I will not allow these people to be betrayed.'

This was the signal for an ambitious spending spree. For most managers the option of buying an international is not available, because the majority of clubs do not have the money to invest in a top player, but for the boss of United it has become part and parcel of the job. Sexton had spent nearly £3.5 million and this was soon surpassed by his successor.

Supporters always enjoy debating the merits of a manager's transfer policy and over the years United's various bosses have made bargain signings and errors in the transfer market. For a manager, it is a source of immense satisfaction to make a good signing, because it one of the truest tests of his judgement. For Atkinson, this part of the job also provided him with the opportunity to create the sort of attacking team he had always dreamed of building.

'I have a dream team in mind'

Ron has probably got where he has in the game because he is a bit of a gambler and this makes him a bold manager in transfer dealings, because he is prepared to put his reputation on the line. At West Brom he built, without lavish funds, a side full of the artistry he prizes so highly. Derek Statham, Peter Barnes, Cyrille Regis, Laurie Cunningham and Len Cantello would have graced any team in the land.

When he took over at Old Trafford he was explicit about his intentions: 'I have a dream team in my head. I don't know if I will be able to get it together completely but I intend to have a damned good try. If I can get all of the men I would like, then only one or two players from the existing team will remain.' In Martin Edwards he found a chairman willing to back his vision of investing in top players to bring success.

Ron nearly signed Brighton's Mark Lawrenson, who, with his Liverpool team-mate Alan Hansen, formed one of the best ever British central defensive partnerships. In the event, only four players — John Gidman, Frank Stapleton, Remi Moses and myself — were signed at the start of his reign.

Norman Whiteside, our hero in the 1985 FA Cup Final, challenges Everton's Pat Van Den Hauwe.

Ron never lost sight of his ambition to put together one of the all-time great teams. If all his signings had come off, then United would have lined up as follows for the 1983 FA Cup Final: Peter Shilton in goal; John Gidman, Gordon McQueen, Mark Lawrenson and Arthur Albiston in defence; a midfield of myself, Ray Wilkins, Arnold Muhren and Glenn Hoddle; with Frank Stapleton and Trevor Francis in attack.

Many of those players, of course, never actually got to pull on the famous red shirt of United. One of the biggest disappointments was that Glenn Hoddle did not sign for the Reds. He might just have won us the championship. The prospect of teaming up with him thrilled Ray Wilkins and myself. We three had played together for the England youth team. Some people dismiss Glenn as a luxury player, but it is bad players who are a luxury. Glenn was one of the finest long ball passers in the game and he had the rare ability of being able to win a match on his own. It would have suited me down to the ground to have been running on to his pinpoint passing, and I am convinced we would have clicked.

Once the sportswriters knew that Atkinson was rebuilding the United midfield, there was a flood of speculative articles including some which claimed, without foundation, that he was bidding for Michel Platini. There was simply no way that United had the financial resources to compete with Juventus for his signature, although it would have been a mouthwatering proposition to have combined with the outstanding player of my era — and my professional idol. Platini would have been a success in the English League, because he could dribble, make space in crowded situations, pass with great vision and had a free-kick technique that was the finest in the world.

Above: **Three of United's longest serving players. Martin Buchan, an inspirational captain, brings the ball out of defence with characteristic coolness, while Lou Macari, to his left, and Arthur Albiston look on.**

Ron had been concerned about some of the flaws in Jimmy Nicholl's defensive game and he made only one substitute appearance under Ron before leaving for Toronto. Mickey Thomas was also soon on his way, in the part-exchange deal that brought Gidman to United. By July 1982 Garry Birtles, Tom Connell, Sammy McIlroy and Paddy Roche had also left.

Atkinson did not approach the job in a scattergun way — it was not change for the sake of change. When he had arrived at United, he had let it be known that he had strong reservations about Gary Bailey, Mike Duxbury, Kevin Moran and Arthur Albiston. After seeing them at close range he revised his opinion and they became an integral part of his plans. Ironically, all outlasted him at the club.

Buchan radiated authority

There had been a mixed look to the squad that Atkinson had inherited. Players had survived from different eras. McIlroy, the last 'Busby Babe', had been given his debut by Frank O'Farrell, and it was O'Farrell who had signed Martin Buchan from Aberdeen. Nicholl and Albiston, former United juniors, had been introduced by Tommy Docherty, who had also signed Lou Macari from Celtic. The bulk of the squad — including Bailey, Birtles, Duxbury, Grimes, McQueen, Moran, Thomas and

Wilkins — had been bought or introduced by Sexton. It was strange playing with some of the Reds' golden greats. I played four games with McIlroy before he left, but even in that space of time it was easy to tell he was an accomplished player.

Several established players were a great help to me during my early days at Old Trafford. I had known Ray Wilkins and his wife Jackie before I moved up to Manchester, but I hadn't had much contact with the other lads. Lou, Gordon and Martin took me under their wings, which definitely helped me settle in.

I learned a lot about captaincy from Martin Buchan. He was a very reserved person, but he played with the full command of his experience and radiated authority on the pitch. If he thought players were showing anything less than total commitment

he would be down on them like a ton of bricks. He was very quick in the tackle and nothing seemed to ruffle him. Lou, however, was a different sort of person. He was humorous, irrepressible and he loved the horses, so we had a lot to talk about. He was confident and creative on the pitch.

I had met Steve Coppell during international duty with England, and he was one of the most consistent players I have ever come across. It is no surprise that Tommy Docherty rates him as his best buy. Steve was an expert crosser of the ball and would wear down full-backs with the sheer intensity of his workrate. He understood intuitively when to make a pass and he had a marvellous shot on him. It was a great loss to England and Manchester United when he was forced into early retirement. Steve is a shrewd

RON'S TRANSFER RECORD

Ron Atkinson explained, in an interview for Glory, Glory Man United!, his initial strategy at United: 'My primary aim was to end the domination of Liverpool. United's team needed surgery, primarily because most of the better players were no spring chickens. Martin Buchan, Lou Macari and Sammy McIlroy were all near the end of great careers and we had also just lost Joe Jordan on freedom of contract to A.C. Milan.

I decided that I would try and get the four players I needed in one fell swoop. I said to Martin Edwards, the Chairman: "It would be great if we could push the boat out with some signings, as it is important that we can get a group of players who will give us real strength." I told him that buying the players in one go meant that we would not have to raid the transfer market for two years — and that is what actually happened.

We needed a striker and Frank Stapleton fitted the bill perfectly. I had been worried about Jimmy Nicholl, and John Gidman gave us more solidity in that full-back position. Contrary to speculation, however, I did not go in for Michel Platini. I did try to sign Glenn Hoddle and I was impressed with his attitude during the talks we held. He was into freedom of contract with Spurs, and we came reasonably close to signing him. I think if he had moved to an English club at that time it would have been to United.

I was disappointed to lose out on Mark Lawrenson. We had virtually agreed a deal with Brighton. They were to get Ashley Grimes, Jimmy Nicholl and cash in return for Lawrenson. In the end, though, they went for a straight money-only deal with Liverpool. At the time we couldn't match that, because it would have used up the bulk of the money we had set aside for Robson's transfer.

I also met Brian Clough to discuss buying Trevor Francis, but I thought he was too great a risk for £1 million. There was even speculation that George Best, who was said to have been included in Northern Ireland's squad for the World Cup qualifier against Scotland, would be rejoining United. Besty, who was 35, had just come back from America and said on a local radio station that he would love to have a crack at playing for United again. Within hours reporters started to ask: "Are you going to sign Best?" I said I would be happy for George to train with us and we would take it from there. It was just a little thing Besty inspired and it fizzled out. Robbo later joked that if I had actually brought him back it would have been as my drinking partner.

I was very concerned about the lack of power in the centre of the team. Robson was my priority. I had been in charge of him at West Brom for about three years and I knew he was a world class player. His ability was not fully appreciated by some other managers. I

said to Martin Edwards: "There is absolutely no way that this signing is a gamble. Manchester United will never regret buying Robson." Nobody could dispute that assessment. Bryan has proved to be the outstanding British player of the 1980s.

At the same time Remi Moses's contract at the Hawthorns had expired and he came to see me in a hotel in Manchester. At the moment, strangely, I was having transfer talks with Stapleton. I was surprised to see Remi, who is a shy sort of lad, and when I asked him what he wanted, he said: "I want to play for you at United!" So I sent him into my bedroom to wait for a couple of hours while I chatted with Frank. In the event, I was pleased to be able to reunite Moses and Robson, because they made such a powerful duo. Remi had an unfortunate time with injuries, otherwise he would have been an England regular for years.

There were other players I negotiated with, including David Mills, Kevin Keegan, Frank Worthington and Charlie Nicholas, and I would like to have bought Alan Brazil in 1983. Missing out on signing him then, when he was at the top of his form, was the biggest mistake I made in those first two years as manager of United.

My transfer record at Old Trafford stands up to scrutiny. I brought Robson, Muhren, Strachan, McGrath and Stapleton to Old Trafford for fair prices, and you couldn't wish to see better players.'

fellow and he went on to great things. After being Chairman of the PFA, he has enjoyed a good measure of success as the manager of Crystal Palace.

That 1981-82 season was one of experimentation for the manager and his new players. Transfers are never a sure-fire thing, because no matter how good they are, there is always a question mark about how well players will cope. Frank Stapleton, who was bought from Arsenal, had no trouble on that score. He was ice cool dealing with pressure and accepted responsibility. Frank took his fair share of knocks, but in six seasons at United he clocked up 286 appearances. He was superb with his back to goal and when you played a ball to him you knew the return would be perfect. He was a really hard trainer. Frank, myself and Norman Whiteside would stay behind after training for extra heading practice, which improved my technique no end, was great fun and definitely sharpened our goalscoring instincts.

Because of our training sessions I had been aware of the shining potential of Whiteside, a teenager from Belfast. Ron Atkinson has always looked to promote youngsters from within if they are good enough and in April 1982, at Brighton, he introduced Whiteside as a substitute. Norman, who was over six foot and weighed 12 stone, said he was 16, so I demanded to see his birth certificate. The first thing he did was go in among the Brighton players in their wall and make room for himself. That summer, aged 17, he was selected for the Northern Ireland squad and became the youngest player ever to appear in the World Cup Finals, breaking a 24-year record held by Pele.

Norman had wonderful touch, and in the next few seasons he was on a par with the skill level of Kenny

Dalglish. Norman had the same wonderful ability to shield the ball, turn and shoot in one quick, fluent movement. It left defenders in a real quandary about how close they should get to mark him, because they knew that he could leave them for dead with one body swerve. I never saw an opponent who intimidated him — it was usually the opposite. Steve Coppell nicknamed him 'Gripper', after the school bully in the television series *Grange Hill*.

Muhren suited me perfectly

Aggression was a vital part of Norman's game, but it should not obscure his skill, vision and passing ability, and the fact that he had the character to cope with what happened to him at such an early age. He proved that he possessed the temperament to get the best out of his abilities and Norman was always a player for the big occasion. He scored in two FA Cup Finals, a League Cup Final, an FA Cup semi-final and a Cup Winners' Cup semi-final. It was very sad that injuries forced him to retire in his mid-20s.

In March 1983 United got an absolute bargain in Paul McGrath — who cost £25,000 from the Dublin club St Patrick's Athletic. When Paul first arrived he was somewhat careless about his play. Atkinson dubbed him 'Dolly Daydream' because of his laid-back style. A few of the players, myself included, talked things over with Paul during a quiet drink and explained that his concentration was letting him down and why we thought he was not doing himself or the team justice. Supportive team-mates will always try and get the best out of a colleague and the ideal time to have a chat with someone is informally. If you have a few players together having a few pints they will come out with things that might be too personal to say at a formal team talk on the club's

Top: **Arnold Muhren, the Dutch midfield ace, plays a typically graceful pass with the outside of his foot. Arnold was one of the finest passers in football, while Remi Moses (*opposite*) was a tigerish competitor.**

Peter Beardsley and his wife Sandra model a United shirt. Peter came on loan, but got to wear the shirt in only one first-team game — a Milk Cup tie in October 1982 — and he was substituted for Norman Whiteside.

premises. There is no point in criticising for the sake of it, but it can be done constructively, which is what happened with Paul, and he was grateful for our concern. Once he realised his own potential he toughened up physically and mentally, and developed very quickly into a player of world class ability.

Paul played 163 League games in eight seasons at United. Without checking the record books I would probably have lost money on a bet about that. If I had been asked how many matches Paul missed for United, I would never have guessed in the region of 200 games, which just goes to show what rotten luck he had. I once said that Paul was the best player I had played with. He had unbelievable pace, was equally at ease playing a pass with his left or right foot, read the game well, was cool under pressure and powerful in the air. He had everything. I would probably rank Paul Gascoigne above him now, but that in itself shows how highly I rate McGrath.

One of Atkinson's best buys was Arnold Muhren, who arrived on a free transfer from Ipswich Town. To get a player of his class for nothing was a remarkable deal. His style suited me perfectly. In his two full seasons at the club I scored 33 goals, and many of those goals were the result of Arnold's selection of pass as I broke forward. He had such perceptive passing skills and he introduced a superb element of composure into our play, something that had been bred into him at Ajax during his time there in the early 1970s. It was enlightening to hear his views on football. He had kept himself fit and was sold too soon by United. He proved that in the excellent way he performed for Holland, at the age of 37, in the 1988 European Championships in Germany. Arnold told me that he fancied going into management or coaching when he retired and I am sure he will make a success of any career he pursues.

I rate the United midfield of 1983 as the best of my Old Trafford career. The third member of a brilliant midfield quartet was Ray Wilkins, whose weight of pass was always finely judged, allowing me to get forward knowing that I wouldn't be making a wasted run. When I started at United he was the skipper and he taught me a lot about the art of captaincy. He never panicked and was always encouraging if things were going badly. He broke his cheek bone in October 1982 and I replaced him as United and England captain. When he was fit again, competition for midfield places was intense and he was left out. He said: 'I'll play anywhere to get back, even in goal.' Many people thought this would make us rivals, but he was, and has remained, a close friend. A poser would have thrown a tantrum and demanded a transfer, but Ray stuck at it and won back his place.

He was unfairly described as a boring player, an image that was cemented when Atkinson called him 'the crab' because, Ron joked, Ray only ever moved sideways. Ray strikes the happy mean between boldness and caution. He likes making constructive passes, but he does not believe in giving away possession and people branded him with the 'boring' tag because he would rather play a holding pass, to keep the ball with his own team, than play a hit-and-hope pass. His consummate reading of the game is the reason he was a success in Italy and has remained a fine player well into his 30s with QPR.

Ron created a splendid midfield

United also had Remi Moses in midfield at that time. He was a driving force, but his hard man image was unfair and detracted from his abilities as a creative player. He gained this reputation because he used to mark key players and harry them out of their stride. He was a tigerish competitor and one of the most unselfish footballers I have ever played with. Creating such a splendid midfield was one of Atkinson's finest achievements. Finding the right blend of players is like completing a hard jigsaw puzzle — sometimes a piece won't fit until you have the other pieces in place — but he was very gratified that his painstaking plans worked out.

Ron has come in for stick about missing out on players or making poor buys — and some of his signings did fail to make their mark. Peter Bodak, who came on a free transfer from Coventry, was one such example. One criticism that has been levelled at Atkinson is that he was at fault in not seeing the potential of Peter Beardsley and David Platt. In an interview for this book, Atkinson said: 'Beardsley had signed on loan from Vancouver Whitecaps in September 1982 and was doing fairly well in the reserves. Brian Whitehouse, our reserve coach, said he would sooner stick with Mark Hughes, because he thought he was a better player. 'Sparky' had proved

Opposite: **Paul McGrath heads clear from West Ham's Tony Cottee during United's 2-0 win at Old Trafford in August 1985. Paul is one of the most talented footballers I have ever played with.**

his worth in the juniors and came free, whereas Vancouver wanted about £500,000 for Beardsley, which was a hell of a lot of money in 1982. That was the deciding factor really. I can remember telling Peter that if the Canadians came back with a reduced demand then we would be happy to take him. In a funny way, though, if he had actually stopped at United his career might never have taken off. When he eventually went to Newcastle, he didn't have the pressure that lads face at Old Trafford, where they are expected to do well as soon as they are given their chance in the first team.'

United had no space for Platt

Beardsley was just dead unlucky at United. Ron had spent a lot of money in his first season and Hughes had started to come good. At first, there was talk of a figure of around £200,000 for Beardsley, which would have been an absolute bargain. Then Vancouver increased their price. Even though Peter had been playing for the reserves he trained with the first team and his talent was striking. We all hoped United would sign him, but it came down to money.

The David Platt situation was different. He was in the reserves trying to make a breakthrough, but he caught Ray and myself, England regulars, at the peak of our careers and we were in the centre of midfield, where he played. So no matter how well David was progressing, the Boss could not find a place for him. It is a tough decision for the coaching staff to be able to say with absolute conviction that a promising player will blossom into a certainty. They did not

have the benefit of hindsight. Within a couple of years the space was there for him, because Ray had moved to A.C. Milan. Now, it would cost about £7 million to bring David back!

There were other pieces that Ron had tried to fit into the jigsaw. In March 1983 he acquired the late Laurie Cunningham on loan from Real Madrid. I had played with Laurie at West Brom and his dazzling ball control and turbo acceleration made him one of the best in the world. He played five times for United, and scored a tremendous overhead kick against Watford, but Laurie was never fully fit during his stay and the proposal to get him permanently never came off.

During the next season Ron thought he needed more firepower and he took Garth Crooks on loan from Tottenham. Crooks did a fair job for the team, scoring twice in seven games, but he said he felt like 'a trespasser'. It was difficult for players on loan to do well then, because the team was going through a transitional period, when Ron was trying to find a better blend. However, some stop-gap signings, such as Arthur Graham and Peter Barnes, did work out.

When a manager has players flitting in and out of a team he needs others who are models of consistency. At United, throughout the 1980s, Mike Duxbury was such a player. In one exhausting season he played all 60 games, and he deserves a medal for that feat alone. He was a local lad, a model professional and his versatility was a real strength. There was

Below: **Jesper Olsen, making his League debut for Manchester United in August 1984 against Watford, teases Lee Sinnott. Olsen was a prodigiously skilled winger but he never fulfilled his potential at United.**

never any need to spur him on. His favourite position was midfield, but more often than not he ended up in defence, usually at right-back, but Duxbury played well enough there to earn 10 full international caps in that position.

Another model professional was Arthur Albiston. He had outstanding natural ability and possessed great stamina. It meant that he could keep up with the fastest wingers throughout a game and was never given a roasting, which is a good litmus test for any full-back. He knew when to calm things down and he always looked for the intelligent pass to feet.

United also had its share of battlers and none more so than Kevin Moran. He was so brave that he picked up some terrible head injuries and there was a joke at one point that Kevin had more stitches in his head than in his suit. He was a terrific reader of the game and strong in the air, although he was often giving away a few inches to his opponent.

These players were permanent fixtures during Atkinson's five years at United, but after three full seasons, Ron built a new team. Using the money from the sale of Ray Wilkins, he bought Gordon Strachan, Alan Brazil and Jesper Olsen. Gordon had originally been surprised to be pencilled in as a wide player on the right, but Atkinson was reverting to the type of team seen in the days of Coppell and Hill. The fans appreciated the return of wide men, and there is no denying the verve of Ron's 'second' team.

Above: **Arthur Albiston controls the ball with his usual efficiency. Albiston made his FA Cup debut in the 1977 Final and went on to collect two more winners' medals with United, in 1983 and 1985.**

'The team was like a toy to Ron'

Of this talented trio, Gordon, who cost £600,000 from Aberdeen, proved to be the best buy. He was very good for dressing-room morale, and a wizard on the pitch. He had such a range of skills, and was so inventive, that he gave us tremendous variety going forward. Gordon had the vision to hold the ball when the pass was not on, and the ability to beat his marker. He could not be a dull player if he tried.

Olsen had been expected to create the most dramatic impact. Atkinson said of the Dane: 'Jesper will become the biggest playing sensation at Old Trafford since George Best.' Olsen was one of those wingers who head straight towards goal the moment they receive the ball. He never really concentrated on the defensive side of the game. Wingers like Steve Coppell, who consider their covering responsibilities to be a priority, only come along once in a blue moon. When you get a natural worker on the flanks it takes such a weight off the midfield and full-backs.

When wingers do neglect their covering duties, then the compensation should be that the attacking side of their game is truly exceptional. In training, Olsen was probably the the most gifted player I have seen; he was able to beat five players in the same run. But there were too many competitive matches when he faded from the game; he would give one sparkling performance in five, and never lived up to his potential, scoring only 24 goals in 175 games.

After the 1983 League Cup Final the manager had decided that we needed impetus in the forward position and he tried to sign Ipswich's Alan Brazil,

but he went to Spurs. 'Alan Brazil is to goalscoring what Robson is to midfield play,' Ron Atkinson said later. In December 1983 United's fans had seen Alan score a spectacular overhead goal at Old Trafford for Spurs and they were enthusiastic when he arrived in 1985. By then, however, Hughes was red-hot and claiming the striker's position. Alan never had a long run of games and when he did get his chance a bad back problem blunted his impact.

Midfield players were Ron's badge of honour in the transfer market, but he was less successful at signing forwards. Hughes had proved himself a gem of a player and it is fair to say that Ron never really replaced Mark when he was sold to Barcelona. Atkinson bought Peter Davenport from Nottingham Forest and although he was a fair player, United's supporters contrasted him unfavourably with the aggressive, no-holds-barred approach of Hughes. Another signing, Terry Gibson, didn't really cope with the expectations at United. He scored only once in 23 games and was soon sold by Alex Ferguson.

These are minor blemishes when viewed against the overall success of Atkinson's transfer policy. Gordon Strachan once said: 'The team was like a toy to Ron, something he created to give himself pleasure as well as bring United success.' That had been Ron's aim when he arrived at Old Trafford and no one could dispute that his Manchester United teams were successful — and entertaining.

ALEX ARRIVES

The Alex Ferguson who arrived at United in November 1986 was the most sought-after manager in Great Britain because of his achievements in his eight years at Aberdeen. He engineered little short of a revolution in the game north of the border, one of the most remarkable feats of management in the British game. Between 1970-71 and 1978-79, every League title and Scottish Cup was won by either Rangers or Celtic: Ferguson's Aberdeen proceeded to shatter that domination. He led them to the championship three times, the Scottish Cup four times, the Skol Cup once, the European Cup Winners' Cup, the European Super Cup and the Drybrough Cup. In addition, they were runners up in the League twice.

Of course, the string of successes at Aberdeen was the result of more than the abilities of one individual. Ferguson had an excellent number two in Archie Knox, who had joined him from Dundee, and the team he inherited from the outgoing boss John Greig was an excellent outfit, with many of the players in their mid-20s and moving into their prime. Willie Miller and Alex McLeish were the defensive rocks on which the whole side depended, while on to this solid central defence were grafted the marvellous ball skills of Gordon Strachan, Peter Weir and Mark McGhee.

Yet there is no doubt that Ferguson was the catalyst who released the talent on the field. His departure was a 'shattering blow' according to the son of the Chairman, a former United player, and the club has never recovered its previous eminence in Scottish football. Aberdeen were paid £60,000 compensation for Ferguson (he still had two years of his contract to run there) and, at 44, he was the fourth Scot of the club's eight managers since the war. As he put it: 'Manchester United are the only club I would have left Aberdeen to join. It was a great wrench to leave Pittodrie, but I recall the late Jock Stein once telling me that the biggest mistake he made was to turn down Manchester United and I vowed I wouldn't do the same.'

I follow most of world football and was well aware of how impressive Alex Ferguson's record had been at Aberdeen, and didn't realise that he was the Board's first choice, however Bobby Charlton later told me that the directors had had him in mind for some time — but then so had the Boards of other top clubs: Wolves, Rangers, Arsenal, Tottenham Hotspur, and Aston Villa in the UK alone, and Barcelona at the head of the list from abroad, had all at least considered making a serious offer.

The team had started the 1986-87 season badly under Atkinson, winning only one of the first nine

Alex Ferguson, flanked by his assistant Archie Knox, keeps us on our toes during the 0-0 draw at Charlton in February 1987. His comments may have been directed at me — I missed a penalty in that game!

FERGUSON'S FINE PEDIGREE

The son of a Govan shipyard worker, Alex Ferguson was a strong character from his youth, always prepared to stand up for what he believed in: as an apprentice toolmaker in his teens he organised his fellow apprentices in industrial action, for example. His playing career took him through Queen's Park, St Johnstone, Dunfermline, Rangers (for whom he signed in July 1967 at a fee of £65,000, then a record between two Scottish clubs), Falkirk and Ayr United. As a goal-scoring inside forward he was Scotland's highest scorer in the 1965-66 season, and his 31 League goals for Dunfermline in that season remains a club record. But he was also a bustling, competitive player, who at one point was sent off for fighting (with Colin Stein, later a team-mate at Rangers). Ferguson was always prepared to put his own point of view — one of the main reasons he left Rangers was because of a row with manager David White about whether he (Ferguson) should have been marking Celtic's Billy McNeill when Celtic scored the opening goal. At Falkirk he was player-coach for a time, and when injury brought his playing career to an end he was bent on a managerial post, as he told the Ayr Advertiser: 'I feel sure that I've had enough playing experience to have a shot at being a manager.' Perhaps it was because he won no representative honours as a player that he was so determined to succeed as a manager.

He started in management at East Stirling, but soon moved to St Mirren, where his enthusiasm and hard work (he toured the town on match days with a loud hailer, encouraging fans to come to watch) saw attendances rise from an average of 1000 to near 10,000. He pushed St Mirren into the Premier Division, but was then sacked for 'unpardonable swearing at a lady on club premises' according to the directors. He moved on to Aberdeen where he triumphed in the most successful fashion.

When Manchester United lured him south he had already been offered posts at other clubs, including Wolves and Rangers, and had taken the Scottish national squad to the World Cup Finals of 1986. But would the determined aggression that had proved such an asset in the booming northeast of Scotland pay equal dividends in the northwest of England?

Left: John Sivebaek, the Danish full-back, made 20 of his 34 appearances for United under Ferguson before being sold to St-Etienne. He was a fine athlete but had trouble coping with the British style of play.

League games and getting knocked out of the League Cup. It was clear that the team was not functioning properly, and the title was out of reach with the season barely under way. In addition, in spite of the sale of Hughes to Barcelona, the club's accounts had revealed a £1.5 million loss on transfer deals.

When it was announced that Big Ron was leaving, there was no delay in naming his successor: Alex arrived at the club within a day or so of Ron going. Alex was very good on that first day. He called all the staff together at the Cliff training ground and said: 'I have made no decisions. You are all Manchester United players and I will give you all the chance to prove that you are worth your place at the club.' He couldn't have put things in a fairer way. Then, within 18 hours of having flown down from Aberdeen, he was out organising a practice match. Alex realised he had a lot of work to do, as he told the Press: 'This is a big, big job for anybody, but I'm not in awe of it. There's a lot of work in front of me and there will be pitfalls, but I'm not afraid of it...I won't be satisfied until the European Cup is back at Old Trafford.'

The first game under Fergie's control was lost 2-0 at Oxford on 8th November, and the second brought a 1-1 draw at Norwich. Our new Boss went on record as saying that the club was capable of winning the League if everyone put their hearts into it: 'We are still capable of winning the title this season. The players must think this way too. We don't have time to wait for things to happen.' But the problem was consistency. In December, for example, we gave away two-goal leads to let Spurs and Aston Villa hang on for draws; and then, after a terrific display on 27th December, when we won 1-0 at Anfield, we lost by a single goal at home to Norwich the next day. Again, a great performance to beat Arsenal and end their run of 22 games without defeat was followed by a limp display in the FA Cup to lose 1-0 to Coventry, the eventual winners. That defeat meant we had no hope of a trophy, and there were some poor games, including a 4-0 defeat by Spurs.

The season wasn't helped by the poor state of the Old Trafford pitch, which was heavily sanded; the Board decided to change the undersoil heating as a way round the problem, but the condition of the pitch is a difficulty that is proving very hard to overcome! Even though we lost five home games that season, however, it was our away form that was really the problem: we won only once away — in that fine game against Liverpool — drew 11 and lost nine. We finished 30 points behind the champions, Everton.

I had missed a lot of games at the beginning of the season through a hamstring injury, and in all I was unable to turn out on 15 occasions. There were rumours that my career was going to come an end through injury, and Fergie tried hard to stamp that out. It's often difficult for a manager to come down to a big club where there are established stars, and it was a hard situation for him because he was coming down and had to work with a captain who was well established at the club. We hadn't known each other at all before he arrived, and whereas I knew what my attitude would be and that I would have no problems giving him the commitment he wanted, I think he needed a bit of time to get to know and trust me.

'Nobody escapes the wrath'

Of course, there were lots of rumours about a new regime at Old Trafford, with Fergie having a reputation as a quick-tempered disciplinarian. He once made four young players at Aberdeen sing nursery rhymes: 'If they act like children, I treat them like children,' was his comment; he hasn't had any of the lads doing that at Old Trafford — yet! Gordon Strachan gave the squad some details on the new boss's legendary outbursts of anger. He has described how 'Nobody escapes the wrath of Fergie...' and some of us reckoned that if half we heard was true then if we could shoot as straight as the new manager could throw cups then we'd walk away with every competition in sight!

But a lot of what was said was sheer Press exaggeration. As Kevin Moran put it: 'There had been one or two little mishaps towards the end of Atkinson's reign and virtually all the media jumped on the bandwagon categorising Fergie as a strict disciplinarian and fitness fanatic. Within three

Right: **Gary Bailey, who made 373 appearances for United, was forced to retire at the age of 29, because of a knee injury, when he was starting to reach his peak. His loss was a blow to Alex Ferguson's plans.**

months we were supposed to have been fitter than we had ever been in our lives...but he never came in and laid down new, rigid disciplinary structures. When a new man comes in the Press just look for something to hang an image on.'

Alex has no time for sentiment

At first we thought from Alex Ferguson's reputation that he was going to be very strict, but with the older pros he treats us like adults, and the players respect him for that. Nevertheless, Alex didn't let players get away with things when he felt they were in the wrong — he fined Moran, Strachan, McGrath and Garton for being late on to the team bus in March 1987 in Dublin and then fined McGrath and Whiteside for drinking during a tour of Malta in May 1987.

Where the Boss is especially keen on discipline is for the younger players, and he tries to stamp that in. They have to be clean-shaven and have smart haircuts, which is a policy I agree with — they are representing the club, after all. In this, he was definitely much harsher than Ron Atkinson. He also

insisted on the older players looking smart and wearing club blazers on away trips. Without making too much of a point of it, he got the results he wanted — Graeme Hogg's blond streaks soon disappeared, for example.

Where he also differed from Atkinson was in his approach to team selection. No matter who you are, Alex will pick his team to win the next game. He has blinkers on as far as that is concerned and he doesn't give a thought to sentiment or what the player is expecting. He will do what he thinks will win the game for the club. He proved, with Jim Leighton in the 1990 FA Cup Final and with Neil Webb in the Cup Winners' Cup Final a year later, that he will do it even in the biggest games. I don't think, actually, that there is a single player at the club who hasn't been dropped on one occasion at least..

Where Fergie did very well in this early period was in bringing down his number two at Aberdeen, Archie Knox. He really impressed me — he gave great support and was brilliant at training, because he's a jolly type of man and he had so many options in training that he kept it interesting all the time. He made training happy, which is crucial, because you have to be able to enjoy it, and he made sure that the lads had smiles on their faces and maintained a good spirit. Moreover his thinking about the game was very astute and he wanted to see the game played right. The Boss knew he could trust him implicitly.

Because he could trust Archie, Alex was able to feel more secure. Any manager has to trust his staff — his kit man, physiotherapist, youth team trainers, reserve team trainers — because they get to hear all the inside talk in the dressing room. Alex certainly wouldn't have had much — if any — contact with the Old Trafford backroom staff before he arrived, and so having Archie as his assistant was essential. Some managers decide to clear out a whole backroom team when they arrive: that's what happened at West Brom when Don Howe took over. But Alex was very fair to the staff already at Old Trafford. He wanted people who knew and loved United and he gave them a chance to show they were happy to work under him.

'I am not a hatchet man'

For the players, a new manager is also a worry. What differences will it make for them personally? As soon as Alex arrived, the papers were implying that McGrath, Whiteside and myself would be leaving, and there were the usual rumours about injury forcing my retirement. Alex was always very straight and supportive, telling the Press that he thought I was a key member of the side, and when he played me as sweeper I accepted that he was doing a bit of experimenting, seeing how he could improve things.

The Boss was trying to learn how people played and what their best positions were.

Those first six months were a case of suspended judgement all round. The players couldn't really appraise the manager at that time because he was trying to get used to everything around the club. He knew everyone at Aberdeen down to the tea ladies and the cleaners, but there's no way you can operate like that at United. It took him six months to a year to understand how big the club was. But he had the character to master the situation and he worked incredibly hard in his first two years. He grafted and took hard decisions, most of which came off.

Even after the first, rather disappointing six months in charge, Ferguson did not make wholesale changes. 'Forget the stories about a mass clear-out of players,' he told the Press, 'I am not a hatchet man going to axe people. Any reductions in the squad will be done in a civilised way when it is also in the player's interest.' He had, however, reduced the ranks of the youth squad by giving seven junior players free transfers in spring 1987; and five players, including Peter Barnes, Frank Stapleton and John Sivebaek, had left to join other clubs.

Perhaps the worst loss was Gary Bailey, the talented goalkeeper who was in the frame for the England team. Injured the previous season, he managed only two games under Ferguson before breaking down and being forced into premature

Right: Peter Barnes, a former colleague at West Brom, made only four appearances under Alex Ferguson before rejoining Manchester City. *Left:* Frank Stapleton is challenged by Liverpool's Gary Gillespie and Nigel Spackman during our 1-0 victory at Old Trafford in April 1987. We had been going through a bad run during Ferguson's first six months in charge, especially away, but 54,103 fans watched us raise our game to beat our Merseyside rivals. Stapleton, who came on as a substitute that day, played only one more game for United before his free transfer to Ajax in July. A lack of goalscoring power was one of the manager's chief causes of concern during his start at the club, and during the summer break he negotiated to buy Celtic's Brian McClair.

retirement at 29 — a striking example of how fragile is a footballer's career.

There were two major signings that summer: Viv Anderson from Arsenal and Brian McClair. Alex went to a transfer tribunal for both these players, being unwilling to pay either club their asking price but wanting the players. McClair was to be a stalwart of subsequent United teams, and a bargain at the £850,000 the tribunal decided was a fair price. Brian, or 'Choccy' as he is known at the club, had scored 41 goals in 57 games in his final season with Celtic. We had needed a natural goalscorer for some time and Brian looked tailor-made for this role.

During the pre-season break, there was also an intriguing attempt to buy the Swedish international defender Glenn Hysen, but he went to Fiorentina, just when everything seemed arranged. Two years later United tried for Hysen again, but he went to Liverpool. In the event, things worked out well for United, because Steve Bruce, bought the following season, eventually filled that hole in the team, and Hysen had trouble coping with the English game.

These transfer dealings were the first evidence of Ferguson's desire to reshape United along his own lines. Even so, he had been even-handed with the staff he had inherited, letting us know that the opportunity was there to prove our worth. The new manager summed up his start: 'My first six months have been very informative. I have been delighted by the response of the players, there is nothing they cannot achieve if they develop a belief in themselves and are prepared to fight for success. But no one is going to put it on a platter for them.'

SECOND BEST

United's preparation for the 1987-88 season could hardly have been better. We had an enjoyable pre-season tour of Sweden and Denmark, during which the Boss had tried out a new attacking system — using Brian McClair or Norman Whiteside to spearhead the attack, with the other dropping off just ahead of the midfield — which had been a success, and Viv Anderson had proved himself a cheery and talented newcomer. Jim McGregor, our physio, reported the entire squad fit for the start of the season, boosting our feeling of confidence.

United opened the season at the Dell. Norman scored twice, and Danny Wallace caught the Boss's eye with a pair of fine goals for Southampton in a 2-2 draw. My hopes of having an injury-free season took a knock, literally, when Kevin Bond kicked me in the face, breaking my nose, as he was trying to clear the ball, but I managed to carry on playing.

By end of August, with five games played, United were unbeaten, top of the League and our self-belief seemed well founded. Brian McClair had already scored three times, boosting his confidence and putting an early end to any Garry Birtles-related jokes. Optimism was high among the fans: 250,000 people had watched United's first six home matches.

In September and October our encouraging start began to unravel because of inconsistency and we dropped out of the top four. Alex Ferguson had wanted a settled side of Walsh, Anderson, Duxbury, Moran, McGrath, Moses, myself, Strachan, Olsen, Whiteside and McClair, but this 11 played only four games before it had to be altered, and the chopping and changing knocked our confidence.

My shoulder operation in the summer of 1986 had been a complete success leaving me worry-free about it after the surgery. I missed only four League games in 1987-88. In October, though, against Norwich, I met McClair's cross at the far post, headed the ball cleanly and scored, but fell awkwardly and rammed my elbow under my ribs. It knocked the stuffing out of me. With any other player it would not have been news, but it was blown out of all proportion, because people initially claimed my shoulder had gone again.

A week later, in the 1-1 home draw with West Ham, we did suffer a real and crushing injury blow, when Paul McGrath sustained a knee injury which required surgery, and kept him out for nearly five months. Paul had been like a rock in defence and Ferguson later described McGrath's injury as: 'The turning point of the whole season for United.'

In November, on the Boss's first anniversary at Old Trafford, United were in fifth position. When he had taken over we had been 15 places lower, and Alex had achieved this turnaround with the same players. That anniversary came near our 1-1 home

Brian McClair became the first United striker to net 20 League goals in a season since George Best.

draw with Liverpool, the pace-setters, providing our hardest test to date. Whiteside equalised Aldridge's headed goal by putting the ball straight through Grobbelaar's legs and Liverpool were forced to hang on in the face of a strong United assault. We were all bitterly disappointed after the game, because we knew we had let them off the hook. It would have been a crucial time to have closed the gap.

In those first 12 months, there had been constant speculation about the imminent arrival of new players. Alex Ferguson himself said: 'Since coming here I've been linked with 119 players through the newspapers, and I've only bought two.' In December, however, he made one of the key signings of his reign, buying Steve Bruce, Norwich City's captain, for £825,000. The transfer dealings with Carrow Road had not gone smoothly and United nearly pulled out of deal. But the Boss persevered because he knew that there was a real gap in the heart of defence, because of McGrath's injury, and even though he had tried a host of combinations, there was an obvious need for an old-fashioned ball-winning centre-half. Bruce fitted the bill exactly.

Bruce is a born United player

Steve is one of those people who possess the strength of character to be a successful Manchester United player, because he does not allow pressure to bother him. He is a confident lad, enjoys playing and goes out with the attitude that if he does his best that is as much as he can do. He is very committed player, and sometimes it's easier for a player of that temperament to settle in at Old Trafford, because they can channel their determination into the match, and don't have the time or energy to get nervous. He knows what he wants from his team-mates, and shouts his instructions loud and clear. The indecision that had crept into our defence melted away after his arrival.

United ended 1987 on a high note, when Brian McClair scored twice in a 2-1 victory over reigning champions Everton to end the year in fourth place. We were pretty hopeful about making progress in the cup competitions. United gave a good performance at Portman Road in the live FA Cup third round tie with Ipswich Town, triumphing 2-1, with a winner from Viv Anderson, who was not shy at describing the highlights of his goal to us afterwards.

Our display in the fifth round of the League Cup against Oxford United was anything but good. Bruce was cup-tied and it was a frustrating night for him to have to watch us go down 2-0, even though we fought like hell in the second half. It was even more sickening when Oxford went out in the semi-final to the eventual winners, Luton. United bounced straight back and, after beating Arsenal at Highbury in the League, we beat Chelsea in the FA Cup fourth round and then defeated Coventry, Derby and

Right: Viv Anderson, who won 30 caps for England, was Ferguson's first signing. *Opposite:* Kevin Moran, United's Irish defender, outmanoeuvres Chelsea's Kerry Dixon in our 3-1 victory in August 1987.

Chelsea in the League, which took us to second place in the table. Even so, many of our fans and a fair few people at the club believed that our best hope of success lay in the FA Cup.

I had been away with England for a match against Israel and had strained my thigh in training during the trip. I failed a morning fitness test and had to watch the game from the stand. United were very poor in the first half, with passes frequently going astray, and Arsenal were two-up by the break. It did not look as if United would find their cutting edge.

The manager gave the team a kick up the backside during the interval. In the second half we came out raring to go and created chances galore. Soon after Kenny Sansom had cleared off the line, McClair swivelled to net a fine volley. Then, in the 87th minute, Whiteside was tripped, and although the Arsenal players besieged the referee, he stood firm and pointed to the spot. Taking a penalty is never easy, but that particular spot kick was a nightmare. It was right in front of the North Bank, who tried to put McClair off. 'Choccy' knew that his shot would decide the result of the game. He blasted the kick and the ball just scraped the bar as it flew over. A player feels like the loneliest man in the stadium when he places the ball on the spot, and when he misses, he *is* the loneliest man in the stadium, but there were certainly no recriminations against Brian. Out of 11 players, there will be four or five who do

Left: Peter Davenport, signed by Ron Atkinson, races away from Manchester City's Nicky Reid. Peter was a good striker, but he never became a central part of Alex Ferguson's plans. In 1987-88, 13 of his 34 League appearances were as a substitute and he scored only five times. Ferguson's decision to sign McClair indicated that Peter's days at United were numbered. Chris Turner (*opposite*, saving from Arsenal's Alan Smith during United's 2-1 win at Highbury in January 1988), was also an Atkinson buy. He kept goal for the second half of the season, following Gary Walsh's injury, but was replaced by Jim Leighton in the summer.

not want to take a penalty under any circumstances and many others who are reluctant to take on the responsibility, so professionals will never have a go at a colleague who actually has the bottle to take one.

Defeat against the Gunners left a bad taste in the mouth and an uphill struggle for the rest of the season. We had 12 League matches left. Liverpool had gone 26 games without defeat, winning 20 of them, and we knew they would be almost impossible to catch. It is quite demoralising to start a season looking to challenge for the championship or win a cup and then to find yourself in a position where it is unlikely that any medals will come your way.

It took United a couple of games to get the Arsenal depression out of our systems — we drew at Spurs and lost 1-0 at Norwich — but there was no way that we were going let our fans down by allowing the season to peter out. We had the incentive of using the remaining games to polish our playing style. We knew that the Boss would not tolerate slackers; anyone coasting would soon be rumbled and earmarked for an early exit. There is little to equal the motivation of playing for your future at a club.

In March United held second place and had big wins against Sheffield Wednesday and West Ham. Liverpool had been striving to break Leeds' record of 29 League games without a defeat from the start of a season, created in 1973-74. The Everton winner that ended Liverpool's bid, in their 30th game, was scored by Wayne Clarke, brother of the former Leeds striker, Allan. That defeat offered no more than a fleeting glimmer of hope that Liverpool would falter.

There had been constant Press speculation about massive changes at Old Trafford before the transfer deadline at the end of April, but it passed without frenzied activity. The manager said that the media speculation about the comings and goings of players was 'the most worrying aspect of his management', because it made for uneasy relations with his staff.

Paul McGrath and Norman Whiteside had both publicly asked for transfers, but the manager hoped at first that they might still have sparkling futures at the club. At that time Whiteside was only 22. Both had been plagued by injuries that season and the stress and boredom of fighting back to fitness had a generally unsettling effect on them both.

'The laughing stock of football'

Ferguson knew that they were disaffected, but he told them and the fans that it was up to players to prove their worth to the club before asking for new deals. Both players settled their differences with the Boss — albeit in the short-term only. Keeping a big squad happy is a tricky part of a manager's job — particularly injured players and those who are not being selected regularly. Jesper Olsen, for example, who had been replaced in eight games, and 12th man in a further seven, claimed that sitting on the sub's bench had made him 'the laughing stock of football'.

Those players who had gained their chance because of gaps were determined to stake their claim for a permanent place and that kept the team bubbling. On 2nd April we won 4-1 at Derby and McClair netted a hat-trick. Strachan slipped the ball through Peter Shilton's legs, and he told me that the air was blue around the goalmouth as Shilts picked the ball out of the net. Back in the dressing room we were cheered by the news that Liverpool had suffered their second defeat of the season, at the City Ground.

Two days later United faced one of the most important matches of the season — at Anfield. I scored an opener after two minutes, but Liverpool got back into it with goals from Beardsley and Gillespie. McMahon put them 3-1 ahead after the interval, and when Colin Gibson spoke out of turn to the referee he was dismissed. Our 10 men battled like demons, but the game looked beyond us. Then the Boss made an inspired substitution, bringing on Whiteside for Mike Duxbury. Within seconds of coming on he made a crunching tackle on Steve McMahon. Norman always seemed to make those thunderous tackles against Liverpool, and on this day it changed the game. His impetus pushed us on to the offensive and I grabbed another goal.

Following a neat interchange of passes, Gordon Strachan raced through on goal, pursued by Hansen.

He committed Grobbelaar and side-footed the ball home — as cool a goal as you would ever wish to see. Facing angry catcalls, little Gordon strolled over to the Kop, cupped his ear, as if to hear the abuse more clearly, and mimicked smoking a cigar. Then, right at the death, we nearly created a sensation, but McClair missed a splendid chance to make it 4-3. The Liverpool camp, however, were far from happy about the result and after the game there was a bit of a spat between Kenny Dalglish and Alex Ferguson.

The Reds kept up the pressure on Liverpool in April, with wins against Luton and QPR. When Paul Parker later joined us, we reminded him about that game, because he scored a spectacular own goal. In the game against Luton, Brian McClair had broken United's 20 League-goals-in-a-season-hoodoo, which had plagued successive strikers at Old Trafford since

George Best had last achieved the feat 20 years before. Smashing that record was important, because any statistic that is used by people to keep harking back to the Busby days is better buried than available as a stick with which to beat current players. Brian scored 31 goals in all that season, 24 in the League. Some were poaching goals, others long-range shots, there were numerous headers and even a spectacular scissors kick that rated as our goal of the year.

It would be his job on the line

For only the second time since Busby's reign United had finished as runners-up, with 81 points, nine behind Liverpool, but nine ahead of third-placed Nottingham Forest. We had lost only five times, United's lowest number of League defeats since 1909, and we had been beaten once in our last 16 games.

One of the essential ingredients of success is a settled team. Eight Liverpool players had made 35 or more full League appearances that season, compared to only three players, including me, at United. Moreover, a settled defence is at the heart of a successful team. A key to our improvement had been Bruce and McGrath having a run together at the end of the season. In the eight games they started together, United won seven and drew one.

When he reviewed the situation, Alex Ferguson was faced with a stark choice. He could decide either to press on with the players already at United, hoping that they could raise themselves an extra gear to compete effectively with Liverpool, or decide, as he did, that he would have to strengthen the squad

This created a great deal of uncertainty, as Chris Turner later explained: 'A lot of us knew when Alex arrived that he wanted to make changes. There had been a lot of speculation among the circle of players — about seven of us — who were likely to be booted out. Liverpool got off to a scintillating start and if it had not been for that United might have edged it. Nevertheless it had been a good season and some of us were startled that finishing second was regarded as failure. It perplexed us that the players who had helped challenge for the title were to be discarded.'

It is understandable that players were disappointed to have done well and then found that the Boss was looking to buy players in their positions, but those are the tough decisions that a manager is paid to take. Ferguson had been fair to the players, because the entire squad had been given 18 months to prove their worth. Ultimately, it would be his job on the line and he knew that to make the League dream possible United needed a few more players of genuine international quality.

I was on good terms with many of the players he decided to replace, and had enjoyed playing with them, but viewed objectively, I have to say that the team, which was essentially the remnants of

Right: **Here, playing for England in June 1990, I offer a bit of guidance to the brilliant Paul Gascoigne. If Gazza had sought my counsel two years earlier I would have advised him to join Manchester United.**

Atkinson's last team, was not good enough to win the League. It would have been easy for Alex to have rested on his laurels at that stage and maintained the squad, which would probably have come in the top three in the League in 1988-89. But he knew that for United to be in a position to lead British football in the 1990s then a complete overhaul was necessary.

This rebuilding may have started even earlier if circumstances had allowed. Ferguson had tried to buy several players in 1988. Paul Gascoigne was approached during the season. In Bobby Charlton, Gazza had a big fan on the Board. Martin Edwards made a formal offer of £2 million to Newcastle United, but Tottenham's bid proved decisive.

I was extremely disappointed that Gascoigne's move to United fell through. I have been bowled over by his talent. Every aspect of ball control is as natural to him as breathing and he has more confidence in his ability than I have seen in any other footballer. While preparing for the 1990 World Cup there was a lot of time to practice and I really saw his ability in the training sessions then. He doesn't just do circus tricks — he takes his skill into a game. Paul does have an excitable temperament, demonstrated in its worst light in the way he picked up his knee injury in the 1991 FA Cup Final, and I sincerely hope that the devilment in him does not come at too high a price.

If Gazza had come to United in 1988 it would have helped his career. He once said that he was pleased he had gone to Spurs because he thought that he

might have been overawed playing alongside me at United. I think Gazza made the wrong choice. He should have come to Old Trafford. We would have made a fantastic partnership and both our games could have developed. He is a born Manchester United player. Old Trafford would have been the perfect stage and our fans would have loved him.

I am not knocking Tottenham in any sense by trumpeting United's virtues, because I regard Terry Venables as a fine manager and I know that the experienced players at Spurs, such as Gary Lineker, made themselves available to help Paul, but there was only so much they could do. London's suburbs are so extensive that players from the same team can end up living more than 20 miles from each other. When players go their own way after training it is unlikely that they will have time to meet up later.

At Manchester United, in contrast, the players live in more or less the same area, and Gazza would have benefitted from living close to the lads. We would have kept a friendly eye on him. Moreover, the pace of life here is less frantic than in London, and there is less scope for some of the distractions outside football to get a grip on a youngster. Gazza was only 21 when he first went down to Spurs, and hangers-on were attracted to him like moths to a light.

Around the time of the bid for Gascoigne, Ferguson had lined up a marvellous transfer, buying Lee Sharpe from Torquay United. Lee was just a month short of his 17th birthday. At that time,

Sharpe was a player for the future and Ferguson, who knew we had taken in an extremely talented group of trainees that season, had made up his mind that he needed players straight away.

Players Alex had in mind, such as Trevor Steven, would not come cheap and at first it seemed money would not be available. The Boss said: 'I thought I would have the luxury of buying players. I have done a lot of hard work at youth levels but to win the League we need to buy. I am disappointed I haven't had that kind of money. Liverpool have bought the best and what sticks in my gullet is the difference between us.' Kenny Dalglish had been given money to rebuild and his new forward-line had powered them to the title. Between them, Aldridge, Barnes and Beardsley had scored 56 goals. Liverpool ended with a goal difference of +63, 30 better than United.

There was, Alex Ferguson said, a clear choice for the Chairman: 'Martin Edwards is now facing the choice between having a very good team and balancing the books. It is impossible to have both.' The Chairman backed our manager and provided the finance — a decision he has never regretted.

In that close season there was little time for reflection about changes at Old Trafford. I went to the European Championships with England. We lost all three games — although I had managed to score against Holland, the eventual winners — and finished bottom of the group, and I couldn't wait for the next season to start.

FERGIE'S FLEDGLINGS

Alex Ferguson had already asked my opinion about Mark Hughes — 'Sparky' — and I told him how highly I rated Mark. So I was very happy when, on 3rd June 1988, Mark became the only player in postwar years to leave and return to Old Trafford. It was interesting talking to him about playing on the Continent. Spanish football had not been to his liking, because the majority of players stayed behind the ball and he rarely got an early pass. He learned more under Uli Hoeness after he moved to Bayern Munich, where his fitness, touch and movement improved dramatically and his timing of runs into the box became sharper. There is no doubt that Mark came back a better player and he was still only 24. The £1.8 million fee would prove to be a bargain, and it boded well for the new season.

Another close-season change was at goalkeeper. Chris Turner's fast reflexes made him a fine shot-stopper, but there had been a question mark over his ability to deal with crosses. Atkinson and Ferguson had both thought that he was short of a few vital inches in height. This would not have been an insurmountable problem if our outfield team had been full of lofty men, but we had few tall players and could not cope with having a small goalie too.

Alex Ferguson had considered going abroad for a replacement — he looked at the Belgian Jean Marie Pfaff and Russia's Renat Dassayev but, in the event, he signed Aberdeen's Jim Leighton for £750,000. Jim had spent his career in the Premier League but had a proven international pedigree. Before joining us he had kept a record 23 shut-outs in 54 games for Scotland, and then proceeded to keep 21 clean sheets in his first season for us. In 64 League games for the club, Chris Turner had kept only 16, so nobody could argue about the merits of that change.

Arrivals were accompanied by departures. Remi Moses, who was only 27, was forced to quit with an ankle injury that had troubled him for three years. Nicky Wood, three years his junior, retired because of a back injury, while Arthur Albiston left on a free transfer to West Brom and Kevin Moran moved to Sporting Gijon of Spain on a free.

But although we were confident about the new season, we suffered some critical setbacks before it even began. On the pre-season tour of Scandinavia, key members of the squad suffered injuries that dogged us for the rest of the season. Four players — Anderson, Duxbury, Gibson and Whiteside — were sidelined at the start of the League campaign. It is impossible to lose really experienced players at the start of a season and not be affected by it. It threw all our planning out of the window and we were bereft of any real rhythm as the playing began in earnest.

Norman Whiteside was plagued by injuries in his last season at United and played only six League games. Here, he takes on Millwall's Hurlock in April 1989.

Peter Davenport started well, with three goals in three games, but he lasted only two months of the season before being sold to Middlesbrough for £700,000, basically because the arrival of Hughes had made him surplus to attacking requirements. Peter had played 106 games for United, scoring 26 goals, but his easygoing approach had alienated some of the fans and backfired with the manager, who dislikes that attitude. He wants players who look as if they are badly hurt by a defeat. That was not really in Peter's carefree nature, which was reflected in the way he played for the Reds. He was not the type of striker who harried defenders and got stuck in with tackles. The Boss recognised his ability, but thought he did not quite match up to the standards he wanted from a United player.

Encountering 'Fash the Bash'

There were other departures during this first quarter of the season: Chris Turner was transferred to Sheffield Wednesday, Graeme Hogg was sold to Portsmouth. Republic of Ireland international Liam O'Brien joined Newcastle United and Jesper Olsen was sold to Bordeaux. Olsen had been at the club for five years, but in the 1987-88 season he had not convinced Ferguson of his right to automatic selection and had been substituted eight times in 30 starts. He was concerned that this would affect his position in the Danish team. For his part, Alex Ferguson thought that having Gordon Strachan and Olsen in the same team made us a bit lightweight.

Basically, Ferguson had assessed all those players and decided that they were not going to live up to what he wanted. In addition, he needed to recoup money for United and he sold them at advantageous prices, getting £2 million for these players — helping to fund the purchase of Hughes and Leighton.

There was one other arrival in the first quarter — Mal Donaghy from Luton. In the draw against Spurs at the start of October, Paul McGrath had picked up another knee injury. It required surgery and kept him out for 14 games. Hogg and Moran were no longer available as cover, so Ferguson bought Mal. Some of the fans didn't agree with this; Kevin Moran had been very popular and they wondered why a tried and tested player had been allowed to go and then £750,000 was spent on a player around the same age. It took time for the supporters to accept Mal, because Kevin had been such a favourite, but the consistency and dedication he has shown has won them over. Mal had played in two World Cup Finals, he knows the game inside out and it was his experience that the manager was having to pay for.

While all this was going on, the team was struggling to find consistency and we were not performing well. When we drew 1-1 with Aston Villa on 5th November, it was the fifth game in a row

Opposite: **Lee Martin, who joined United as a YTS trainee, made his League debut in August 1988 at home to QPR. Lee, born in Hyde, was one of a crop of good youngsters nicknamed 'Fergie's Fledglings'.**

where we had been ahead and lost a lead within a matter of minutes. In the fourth game of that sequence, United were knocked out of the League Cup in a bruising encounter at Wimbledon. I scored the opener in a 2-1 defeat. The rough treatment didn't end on the pitch. As they were going down the players' tunnel, Viv Anderson and John Fashanu became involved in an altercation that ended with Viv needing three stitches and both players being hauled up in front of the FA, where 'Fash the Bash' was banned for three matches and fined £2000 and Viv banned for a game and fined £750. Because a United player was involved it became a big issue.

United drew all five League matches in November, in a run of nine games without a win. Hughes had been finding the net regularly, but McClair had scored only twice in our first 15 games and there was speculation at the end of November that Gary Lineker would be teamed up again with Hughes (they had played together in Spain). Barcelona boss Johan Cruyff offered Lineker for £2.5 million, but United could not afford it. Buying an out and out goalscorer may have seemed like the ideal answer but our problem was not so much in scoring (we'd netted 23 goals in our first 16 games) but in our general play. It would have been interesting playing with a forward of Gary's vision and pace, because it would have given us the option of hitting passes over defences for him to run on to.

'Liverpool cave in like amateurs'

December came and went with little reason for cheer, although on Boxing Day we beat Nottingham Forest 2-0 at Old Trafford. By the end of 1988 United had used 23 players. Ferguson said that it was the worst injury crisis he had suffered as a manager, and youngsters Lee Martin, Lee Sharpe, Billy Garton, Mark Robins, Tony Gill, David Wilson, Deiniol Graham, Clayton Blackmore and Russell Beardsmore had appeared nearly 80 times between them. Through the horrendous injury crisis, these youngsters, all aged 20 or under, who had been nicknamed 'Fergie's Fledglings', had been given their chances as a matter of necessity. These youngsters sparked a brilliant purple patch that could hardly have begun in more dramatic style.

Although the injury crisis and all the other unsettling factors made it a terrible time to face the reigning champions, the curtain raiser for 1989 could hardly have been more exciting, particularly as the match was live on TV. Liverpool were red-hot favourites to win the title, but we could still take comfort from our fine record against the Scousers: in 18 confrontations between United and Liverpool in the 1980s, United had lost only two.

United's team had an unfamiliar look, with established stars mixed in with Martin, Sharpe and Beardsmore, and during the first half we were soon deprived of the services of Strachan, who hobbled off to be replaced by Robins. McGrath, who came on in the 63rd minute for Martin, could hardly have picked a harder day to make his comeback after three

Left: **Steve Bruce makes a challenge on David Burrows during United's memorable victory on 1st January 1989, while Mal Donaghy and Ralph Milne, two pre-season signings, look on. Kenny Dalglish's team had come to Old Trafford confident that they would beat a makeshift United side, full of inexperienced players. In the event, United fought back from a goal down to win 3-1. England boss Graham Taylor, commentating on the match for ITV, said: 'United were superb. The Liverpool lads look totally shell-shocked.'**

months out of the side: and then, seven minutes later, Liverpool went ahead. Instead of cracking, we raised our game. Our fans set about lifting the team and within a minute we were level. Hughes and Donaghy combined to feed the ball to Beardsmore. His jinking run left Staunton and Ablett stranded and his cross was met by a spectacular scissors kick from McClair. Four minutes later Hughes charged down a clearance and fired past Hooper.

There followed a lovely, flowing movement. My back-heel released Sharpe and his cross evaded Robins but was volleyed home by Beardsmore. It was a delight to win that game in such a fine manner. Liverpool had really fancied their chances of turning over a side with so many youngsters, but in the end it could have been 6-1. Ray Houghton said of Kenny Dalglish's reaction: 'I have never seen Kenny so angry. There was a great deal of shouting, screaming and finger-pointing in the dressing-room. He wanted to know why we caved in like a bunch of amateurs. We journeyed home in almost complete silence.'

Jim McGregor to my rescue

Although we were all buoyed by the display, the game is another example of over-the-top publicity. It had been a good team performance, particularly considering the number of inexperienced lads in our side, but it was only *one* game. Immediately, pundits were saying that the youngsters ensured the club a great future, but us older lads were more sanguine about it all. It is one thing to put on a sparkling display and quite another to do it week in week out. People got carried away and raised expectations too far, putting untold pressure on the youngsters.

Any notions that we were ready to storm to the title were squashed the following day at Middlesbrough. All the lads were drained after that Liverpool game, and having to play with 10 of the same players just 24 hours later was asking too much. We lost 1-0.

Although that defeat dampened our title hopes, we still had high hopes in the FA Cup. In the third round we drew QPR at home, but it was the same stalemate as the opening game and ended scoreless. As I challenged for a ball, I collided with a player and was concussed. I swallowed my tongue and was choking but our physio Jim McGregor came to my rescue. I had severely bruised ribs, but was released from hospital after 48 hours and went to the replay.

In that game United's youngsters had, perhaps, their finest hour. Gill, Martin, Beardsmore, Sharpe, Wilson and Graham all appeared for the Reds in a distinctly unusual line-up. I sat with Viv Anderson on the bench, and during the game our anxiety gradually turned to elation. With 15 minutes left United were 1-0 down. Hughes controlled the ball slid it through to Tony Gill, wearing my Number 7 shirt, and he fired a rocket of a shot past David Seaman. Graham scored our second in a 2-2 draw. Loftus Road is always a difficult ground to come away from with a good result and the lads had played with great style. They were willing to run at opponents and took the game in their stride.

That January we felt pretty positive after four gruelling months. The manager had witnessed the improvement in Lee Sharpe, who he was pretty sure was going to play an important part for the team in the future. That was encouraging. The other youngsters had all coped at a high level in important games. By the end of the month, United had won the second replay against QPR 2-0. I had been ribbed by the lads about my scoring rate during the lead-up to the game, but luckily I had a lovely chance during the match — the ball fell to me on the edge of the area, after a corner. Normally in that sort of situation there are defenders rushing straight in to close you down, but I had a split second to control the ball and pick my spot. We then beat Oxford 4-0 in the fourth round. Sharpe was named Barclay's 'Young Eagle of the Month' and Ferguson Barclay's 'Manager of the Month' for the first time, while Beardsmore and Sharpe earned England Under-21 call-ups.

Although our League form remained erratic, we were still going well in the FA Cup. We scraped into the quarter-finals by beating Bournemouth at the second attempt, in front of 54,222 fans at Old Trafford. This was the furthest we had gone in the tournament under Ferguson. The Boss said that this quarter-final against Nottingham Forest was his biggest game so far as our manager. Cloughie's side were an exceptional cup team that year, and went on to win the Littlewoods Cup and the Simod Cup. Their superb defence of Laws, Pearce, Walker and Wilson absorbed our attacking pressure and they were well supported by Webb, Hodge and Clough in midfield. They are great at defending and counter-attacking and eventually they caught us on the break, when Gary Parker turned home Franz Carr's cross.

We took the game to Forest, and were convinced a Brian McClair shot had gone over the goal-line before Steve Hodge hooked it away, but it was not given. We'd been confident about our chances of winning the trophy, and the manner of our defeat was a real sickener. It was a hard loss to swallow because it was the only thing we had left to go for that season. Although we won our next fixture against Luton, the heart had been knocked out of us. Even the Boss said: 'The season did not just slip away after the defeat against Forest, it collapsed.'

Below: **Here I am lining up a shot against Arsenal in the 1-1 draw at Old Trafford on 2nd April 1989. We gave one of our best performances of the season against the Gunners, who went on to lift the title.**

It was the gloomiest run in to the end of a season I could ever remember. The fans felt the same and attendances shrivelled. When we played Wimbledon in May it was to a half-empty Old Trafford of only 23,368, the lowest crowd for 17 years. The message was not missed, because as players we always want to be playing in a packed stadium — that is one of the best things about playing for United. When that ceases, serious questions have to be asked. The end of the 1988-89 season was without doubt the low point of my time at the club; we had won only 18 out of 48 matches, and the fans were very unhappy.

The Boss shouldered the criticism but he was able to generate a belief that he knew what he was aiming for. I was sure that it was a matter of time before we got it right. I was also reassured because of the brilliant work he and Archie Knox were doing at the youth level. Most mornings I am early into the Cliff and sometimes I like to have a coffee and chat in the coach's room before training, so I knew they were restructuring the whole youth system at the club.

The injury crisis cannot be underestimated. There had been massive disruption: 27 players had been used during the campaign and confidence had ebbed and flowed as a result. Nine first-team players, including many internationals, were out injured at one stage. Our injury jinx had even hit the 'fledglings', three of whom suffered serious injuries.

The season's end saw two major departures from the club. Gordon Strachan left after the FA Cup quarter-final defeat. He had come close to signing for the French club Lens, but changed his mind.

THE BOYS OF 88

Alex Ferguson has overhauled the youth system at the club in a quiet but dramatic revolution. Circumstances had forced the Boss to throw youngsters in, but it took courage to play them. He does not allow young players to get overawed and his understanding of their worries can only have been helped by having a teenage son of his own at United.

The youngsters who showed such startling promise in 1988 were dubbed 'Fergie's Fledglings'. People, very unfairly, compared them with the 'Busby Babes', who were the finest youth team in the history of the game. But that is the burden of United. Arsenal, for example, have produced a crop of fine players, including David Rocastle and Paul Merson, but they were allowed to come through without the glare of massive national publicity.

There are many problems for young players, and while the success stories are appealing, it has not been been plain sailing for Fergie's Fledglings since their rise to fame. For a start, the physical pressure of competing at the top level took its toll. Deiniol Graham broke his arm very badly, while David Wilson fractured his leg after that run in the first team. After recovering both were confined to the reserves and later released on free transfers. Their run of bad luck did not stop there: Wilson was injured after moving to Bristol Rovers and made only three appearances in 1991-92. Graham played only 15 times for Barnsley in the same season. Tony Gill was the unluckiest of all the United youngsters. His career was ended by injury at the age of 21.

Even without injuries, establishing a place can be difficult. Wigan-born Russell Beardsmore (above) had, up to June 1992, played 73 times for United. He earned a cult following among the fans, but has struggled to gain and hold a place. Lee Martin was hailed by Ferguson as our most consistent player after the 1989-90 season, during which he scored the winner in the FA Cup Final, but he picked up a back injury and has had to endure a frustrating two years waiting to get back into the first team.

Mark Robins, the top scorer in the reserves from 1987 to 1991, has also found that his chances have been limited because of the quality of our first-team players. He requested a move in 1992, but was then afflicted with a cartilage injury that required surgery.

It is unlikely that a team of young players can form the basis of a trophy-winning side, however popular they are with the fans. Making the leap from promising youth to First Division regular is the hardest one in football. I have lost count of the hundreds of kids I have seen fade after looking like a potential world beater at 16. Some of the Fledglings may seem to have been unlucky — but the main point is that United's youth policy has started pushing these good youngsters off the production line again. That's why we won the FA Youth Cup in 1992 for the first time since Busby's reign in 1964.

Then, after injury, Gordon lost a bit of sparkle and wasn't performing at the same high level of his form when he had arrived here. At Elland Road he has found his form again. I put that down to the season Leeds had in Division Two. They were better than any one else in that division and Gordon regained his confidence. He won the Football Writers' 'Player of the Year' in 1991, and was a key part of their title-winning team in 1992. If he had stayed at United he might never have recaptured his form.

The other notable departure was McGrath. Many fans were upset to see him go, but there had been differences between him and the Boss. Paul later buried the hatchet: 'I don't blame Alex for what

Opposite: **Mark Robins, the talented forward who had been banging in the goals for the reserves, was one of the promising youngsters who earned their full call-up during the 1988-89 season.**

happened. It was awkward for him with a young footballer like me who was a bit out of control on the drinking side of things — I should have behaved better off the pitch. That's why a lot of it was down to me and only a smidgen of blame could be levelled at Fergie. He decided that it was better for me and better for United if I left. In the end, he was right.'

The loss of these two talented players highlighted the basic problem: we did not have a big enough base of tried and trusted servants. United needed a squad that could ride out injury problems. There was a solid platform to build on, because there were 12 or 13 good players, but we needed that crucial extra four or so to make it into a really powerful squad — and we needed it urgently for the next season's campaign or the fans might stay away for good. One of the biggest tests for a team is how it responds to adversity. United were soon to prove that when it came to fighting back we were very special.

MY FA CUP HAT-TRICK

The tail-end of the 1988-89 season had been a very depressing one. Manchester United had been about five players short of a really good squad and I had been worried about where the team was heading. I wanted to be winning things and that was not looking likely. Even the Gaffer conceded the squad 'was going nowhere'. That was the time, in my estimation, when Alex Ferguson proved his calibre. He told the Press: 'My future is at stake, because to continue as manager of United involves being successful.' He knew, realistically, that he had to win a trophy in his third full season, and he admitted that he had pared the staff too near the bone and had to rebuild. But he also had a deep desire to build his own team, and the Board made money available for him, which was pleasing for him and for me.

The manager had a very clear idea of the sort of squad he wanted to assemble. He needed new central players — 'the midfield had cracked up last season,' Alex said. He had lost Norman Whiteside, who had been playing in the centre of the park under Fergie, and Remi Moses had retired. The Boss also had in mind, even at that time, that he would have to look at my role, and he spoke to me about playing as a sweeper. He thought I might not be able to get up and down the pitch as frequently as before, so he was developing a plan for using me in a different capacity — and bringing in players who could fill that central position, or who would be able to replace me if I kept that role but picked up an injury.

A great start to the season

His prime targets were Norwich's Michael Phelan, who turned down a better financial package from Everton to join United, and Neil Webb. He later added Paul Ince. The Boss signed a range of central players. If you look at them together you will see that he bought strong, physical lads. They are all around the 5'11" mark with good builds. Mike is a superb competitor who reads the game really well; and Neil balances a team. He can release players with a timely pass and has an awareness of where to fill in. At Nottingham Forest he had a record of scoring a goal every three games — a superb one for a midfielder. We had played together 18 times for England and I was more than happy that he joined United. Shortly into the season the Boss filled a hole in central defence (that had existed since the departure of Paul McGrath) with Gary Pallister. Ferguson had had his eyes on Gary for a while. In September 1988, when

Lee Martin, a product of United's youth system, gets ahead of Andy Gray to fire home our winner in the 1990 FA Cup Final replay against Crystal Palace. The win was the perfect way to answer our critics.

we had been at home to Middlesbrough, Ferguson had praised Pallister in his *United Review* column. Gary is a powerful lad, standing 6' 4", and the Boss was so keen to get him that he broke the British transfer record and paid £2.3 million for 'Pally'.

Morale in the squad was lifted by the arrival of such class players, and they showed, in pre-season training, that they could really perform. Our new team-mates showed they could express their abilities in a match, and we couldn't have got off to a better start in the League than to defeat Arsenal, the champions, 4-1. Neil Webb had a glorious debut and scored a fine goal. The only cloud that overshadowed that sunny day was the Boardroom controversy.

On the day before the Arsenal match, a stranger called Michael Knighton had turned up at our Cliff training ground to meet the players, so we knew something was afoot. But all our attention was focussed on making a winning start to the season — players just want to get on with the game and are happy to stay right out of Boardroom politics. We certainly hadn't expected the spectacle of Knighton, who had just 'bought' the club, running on to the pitch before the kickoff, blowing kisses to the crowd and banging the ball into the goal in front of the Stretford End. That display, and the subsequent barrage of publicity, didn't do anyone any favours at the club. It just seemed to trigger resentment against United. In the event, Knighton abandoned his multi-million pound takeover bid, but the high-profile story had lingered on for quite a few months. The affair finally ended in May 1992 when Knighton resigned as a United director to take over Carlisle United.

Although the attempted takeover generated a lot of publicity, the decline that the team went into had

Above: **Mark Hughes volleys home an astonishing goal against Manchester City in September 1989. Sparky's capacity to score such stunning acrobatic goals has made him a favourite with United's fans.**

more to do with the difficulties of blending new players — and as a result of the horrendous injuries we suffered. On 6th September, while playing for England against Sweden in a World Cup qualifier, Webb was carried off with a ruptured achilles tendon. He had played only four games for United. I watched the game on TV and could see instantly from the way he fell in a heap, with no one near him, that it was a terrible injury. When a player is running along and goes down with such an anguished expression on his face then you know it's really serious. It was a real blow to Neil and affected him for two years, because it limited his stretch and he has had to battle to get back his former mobility.

'I felt like some kind of criminal'

Webb's injury made the Boss even more determined to get West Ham's Paul Ince. At the end of August Paul's transfer had been shelved on medical grounds, but after an independent report by a Harley Street specialist he was bought for a down payment of £800,000, rising to £1.8 million on a pay-as-he-plays scheme — £5000 per first-team game. The squad was strengthened even further on 16th September, when Danny Wallace signed for £1.2 million in front of the crowd at Old Trafford. Danny then watched us crush Millwall 5-1 — during the game Mark Hughes scored his third hat-trick for United. Our playmaker was Ince, making his debut, and Lee Sharpe scored his first goal for the Reds. That win came after two defeats and we hoped it would mark a turning point. Four days later we began our League Cup challenge with a 3-2 win at Portsmouth — Ince got two goals and Wallace the other. One of the Pompey players caught me on the side of the leg and when I went for an X-ray, the hospital told me it was a hairline fracture. The Press made a big thing of my quick recovery — I was back for the return leg a fortnight later — but it was possibly just a mis-diagnosis.

During those two weeks off I missed one of the most dramatic games of Alex Ferguson's reign. On 23rd September United lost 5-1 at Manchester City. I went to see the game, unfortunately. Some of our key players were missing (Steve Bruce and Neil Webb were sitting beside me in the stand) and we defended dreadfully. United didn't play at all — although Sparky scored the best goal of the day with a splendid volley — and City hit top form. Even though it was a freak result, it was big blow to lose a derby in such a humiliating way, and it roused United's fans against the team and the manager.

The Boss was certainly trapped in the firing-line, and a short time after the defeat he said: 'Every time somebody looked at me, I felt I had betrayed that man. I felt like some kind of criminal. But that's only because I care about the people who support us. It has been the longest 10 days of my life, an eternity in which I must have gone over the defeat a thousand times.' The Press started a whispering campaign

suggesting that Howard Kendall, who was coming back from Spain, would replace Alex Ferguson. Although people speculated about Alex's position at the time, it was actually Mel Machin, City's Boss then, who lost his job to Kendall that season.

After a couple of scoreless draws, and a resounding 4-1 defeat of Coventry, United lost 3-0 to Tottenham at Old Trafford in the League Cup. We conceded sloppy goals that night and the fans booed the team off the pitch. That was followed by a bad defeat at Charlton. We steadied ourselves with two solid wins, against Forest and Luton, and then went into a terrible slump. We were struggling to fit together the contrasting styles of the big-money signings and players were not looking for the ball as they should have done. It is always the same when lots of new players arrive in one quick sequence. A team cannot develop consistency while players are getting used to each other. It is hard for new players to get to grips with such big changes in their personal lives while at the same time they are having to adapt to a new set of team-mates and a different pattern of play.

Despite these problems, we were capable of raising our game. In the 0-0 draw at Anfield on 23rd December, United played really well and were unlucky not to come away with a handsome victory. I suffered a groin strain in that match and for about

I had to watch our nerve-racking fourth round FA Cup tie at Hereford from the bench, but our 'new' players did the club proud, winning 1-0. *Below:* **Gary Pallister, who had a fine game, clears the ball.**

four weeks the doctors could not find out what was wrong with me. I had spent that month resting and trying to make a comeback, but repeatedly breaking down in training. I went to see a specialist in London in the fifth week and he said I needed a hernia operation. Six weeks had elapsed from the time of the game at Liverpool until my operation and it took me that long to come back after surgery. That was intensely frustrating, losing 12 weeks of a season because an injury had not been diagnosed.

On Boxing Day United lost 3-0 at Aston Villa and had a scoreless draw at home to QPR on New Year's Day. During the winter months, the media pressure on the Boss had been escalating. As recently as September, however, Alex Ferguson had signed a new three-year contract with United. I saw at close hand the sort of strain he was under but he never faltered. People were scathing about his expensive signings, but he knew they would pay off once they had settled in. Ferguson later said: 'The Board were great. They never questioned my motives, or what I was trying to achieve. They supported me at the right time. Martin Edwards refused to say "I'm backing the manager", because he thought that would be insulting to me.'

Ferguson would not have gone

Many reporters claimed that Ferguson's job hung in the balance of the result of our FA Cup third round match at Nottingham Forest. We had gone eight games without a win before the tie at the City Ground, but United went there and beat a very good team — and deserved to. United were always in charge. Journalists often say that it adds to the pressure when a match is live on TV, but that's not true. Once you're out on the pitch you don't even think about the cameras. The only player it might affect would be a youngster playing his first game.

The positive attitude of our players decided the match. The lads were playing for the Boss and there was genuine delight when Mark Robins stooped to head home Hughes's intelligent cross. Even if we had lost, I don't think the Boss would have been out of a job. The Chairman and Board of Directors knew he was working hard to get things right and that was how we all felt inside the club — and they would have given him more time to turn things round. If we had lost that tie then our League results in the last few months of the season would have to have picked up, otherwise the pressure on the Boss would have intensified. The Board should be given credit for the way they backed Alex during a tough period — too many managers are fired after hitting one bad patch.

The next Cup game was a tough one as well. We drew Hereford and lots of people were looking for a Fourth Division giant-killing upset. It was a muddy pitch and the conditions suited them. Moreover, Phelan was missing with an achilles tendon injury, Bruce was serving a suspension and I was still absent. Although United did not play particularly well, we battled through to win 1-0 with a nicely worked goal from Blackmore five minutes from time.

We all thought: 'Well, United must come out of the hat first once', but the fifth round draw pitted us away against Newcastle. Even so, we were relieved that we had avoided a First Division club. If a top-class team has the right attitude it will nearly always come through a cup tie against a lower division club. It was a blustery afternoon but there was a good atmosphere at St James's Park. We gave our best performance of the campaign. We could have scored six or seven — and the win was far more comfortable than the 3-2 scoreline suggests. I watched from directors' box and never felt that we would lose, even though they twice dragged themselves from behind — albeit with one very questionable goal. Danny Wallace played well, scoring a neat goal, and McClair scored our winner with his first goal in 17 games. It shows how bad our run was when a forward of his class does not score for nearly four months.

Getting into the last eight of the FA Cup had been a real fillip, but it had not released our anxiety about United's poor League form. A defeat at Millwall on 10th February would have put United into the bottom three and would have equalled a 60-year-old club record of 12 First Division matches without a win. Our players were raising themselves for the Cup matches, but in coming from behind to win at the Den they showed they could do it in the League, too. That victory pulled us away from the danger zone.

On 3rd March United beat relegation strugglers Luton 4-1. It was our first home win since 18th November, and it gave us great heart for the quarter-final against Sheffield United. It was United's 21st quarter-final since the War, and McClair's winner, his third goal in four games, made it 18 wins in 21.

Our match against Oldham, my first game since 23rd December, ended in a pulsating draw. Earl Barrett opened the scoring after five minutes, netting when Leighton failed to hold the ball. The last thing we had wanted was to give away a bad goal and have to chase the game. Happily, we got level quickly. Webb picked me out perfectly and I timed a run to beat the offside trap. Jon Hallworth got a hand to my shot, but he couldn't stop it. It was great to continue my record of scoring in FA Cup semi-finals: that was the fourth time I had scored in that round.

The best of British football

I was making a lot of forward runs, because we were drawn into an open positive game by Joe Royle's attacking line-up. It was a roasting day, and the amount of running I did in the first half took a lot out of me. I tired in the second half, went dizzy with the heat and just couldn't concentrate, so gave the Gaffer the signal to get me off and I made way for Danny Wallace. Webb and Marshall had scored in normal time, and then two minutes into extra time Danny scored our third. It was murder watching those last 30 minutes, because by then I had cooled down and wished I was back out there. It was end-to-end excitement, the best of British football, and Roger Palmer's 107th minute strike made it 3-3.

The attacking play continued in the replay. Paul Ince gave an inspirational display and hit the post with a cracking long-range drive. McClair put us in front with a tap-in, and Andy Ritchie, an ex-Red, made it all-square. Mark Robins grabbed the extra time winner with a typically clinical finish — he took two touches to control Phelan's cross and passed the ball into the net. It had been a draining night, but his deadly finish was a fitting end to a great contest.

That set up a momentous FA Cup semi-final. We had just won two consecutive League games — against Southampton and Coventry — for the first time in nearly five months. We watched most of the Liverpool-Crystal Palace semi-final, and heard the dramatic finale on the radio while travelling to Maine Road. Everybody was delighted with Palace's victory and it gave us a real lift knowing Liverpool were out.

Above: **Mark Robins heads United's first goal in our win at Newcastle United in the FA Cup fifth round on 18th February 1990. St James's Park is one of the hardest venues to win an FA Cup tie, and the atmosphere that day was electric. The match see-sawed for a while but Manchester United deservedly ran out 3-2 winners. We were drawn away for the fourth time in our run for the quarter-final against Sheffield United. United dominated the game for long periods (*right:* Paul Ince wriggles free of his marker at Bramall Lane), and Brian McClair's goal put us into the semi-final against Oldham.**

Three League wins in March eased our relegation fears, but our topsy-turvy League form continued in April. I had been pleased with my recovery from the hernia operation, but I started to feel a bit sore so was rested for a while and concentrated on doing exercises to strengthen my abdomen. I missed our League game at the City Ground, which was just as well. I listened to it on the radio. The players must have relaxed a bit, which backfired badly — Forest were 4-0 up inside 20 minutes. As I switched off the radio I was pleased I was not trooping off to face the Boss in the dressing room after a defeat like that!

I was fully fit for the FA Cup Final, and although we were confident, our defensive performance was feeble. You can't concede three goals in a Wembley final and expect to win. We fell behind when Jim Leighton was caught in no-man's-land as O'Reilly's header looped over the line. Soon after, Wallace wriggled forward, sent a lovely pass to McClair, and I met his cross with a header that brushed off Pemberton and went past Martyn and into the net.

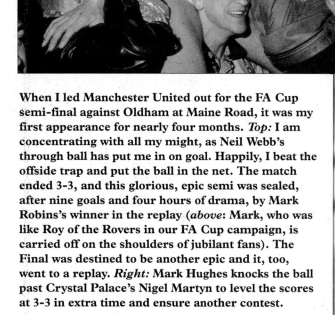

When I led Manchester United out for the FA Cup semi-final against Oldham at Maine Road, it was my first appearance for nearly four months. *Top:* I am concentrating with all my might, as Neil Webb's through ball has put me in on goal. Happily, I beat the offside trap and put the ball in the net. The match ended 3-3, and this glorious, epic semi was sealed, after nine goals and four hours of drama, by Mark Robins's winner in the replay (*above*: Mark, who was like Roy of the Rovers in our FA Cup campaign, is carried off on the shoulders of jubilant fans). The Final was destined to be another epic and it, too, went to a replay. *Right:* Mark Hughes knocks the ball past Crystal Palace's Nigel Martyn to level the scores at 3-3 in extra time and ensure another contest.

United had done well to come straight back, and although we soon got on top, we produced only one goal in this period, a power drive from Hughes, and ended up being punished for failing to build a commanding lead. Ian Wright, the Palace sub, was the catalyst for their revival, but his equaliser was helped by some woeful United defending. We could have got back into the lead, but my header hit the post, and in extra time Wright did well to volley home a John Salako cross that caught Leighton out of position. We showed strength of character, as it was a depressing time to go behind. It would have been easy to let our heads drop, but we completely dominated the last 15 minutes and were rewarded when Hughes calmly finished off an exquisite through ball from Wallace with a precise low shot.

The story of the replay was dominated by Alex Ferguson's bombshell decision to drop Jim Leighton. The squad was informed the night before the game, when the manager said that he had already told Jim and he asked us to keep it a secret, which was fair enough. We all had to concentrate on our own jobs. Everyone felt really sorry for Jim, but the manager had made a tortuous decision — to drop a player for the FA Cup Final, a player who was the club's number one 'keeper and who had appeared in every round. Ironically, as a player, Ferguson himself had experienced the heartache of being dropped for a Final. He was left out of the Dunfermline side that lost 3-2 to Celtic in the 1965 Scottish Cup Final

We may well have won with Jim in goal, but the turning point of the rematch was when Les Sealey, the goalie on loan from Luton who came in for the replay, made a really good save with his feet when the ball flashed through the wall. If that had gone in, Palace could have gone on to win. As it was, we dominated and although Les wasn't in the thick of it that often, those saves he was called on to perform, he made very assuredly — and that gave the lads confidence at the back. Steve Coppell later revealed that Palace had planned to bombard Jim with high balls, and our changed line-up had thrown their

AGAINST ALL ODDS

Archie Knox, in an interview for this book, recalled the 1989-90 season: 'The English First Division was an unfamiliar world to Alex and myself and it took us time to get a grip. We were hit very hard by the extent of the injuries we had during our early period at United. The young players were not a long-term solution — we knew we had to rebuild and to that end we had to buy as a first step.

But that 1989-90 season didn't progress the way we wanted. United are under a microscope, but the off-field dramas triggered even more criticism. As Fergie's assistant I could get on with my work without bearing the brunt of it, but Alex was directly in the firing line. He came through against the odds and there is no better testimony to his character than that. Everyone harped on about the amount of money he had spent, but no one talked about the finance he had recouped.

Whenever we lost, the same old jibes were trotted out, and although it is hard to shut out, the players were resilient — but they would not have got to the heights they had reached in football without developing thick skins.

Even though we were doing good work at youth level, it is the success or failure of the first team that decides a manager's fate. Once we had won the third round tie against Nottingham Forest we felt we had broken through a key barrier. But we had to win the Cup the hard way — and we did.

Of course, in that Final against Crystal Palace the decision to drop Jim Leighton for the replay was the major talking point. The result, and Sealey's performance, prove that the decision was justified. There was no doubting our faith in Jim's ability, but his confidence had taken a real battering in the weeks before. Alex knew he would be judged on his decision and he was proved right. His transfer policy has also been vindicated, and Hughes, Pallister, and especially McClair, have been wonderful signings. The hat-trick of trophies showed that the work Alex and I did in those years was right.

tactics out of the window. Palace knew that if they allowed us to play our passing game they would lose, so they tried to hassle us out of our stride. You expect hard tackles in a Cup Final, but we gave as good as we got; we are not a team to be bullied out of a game. Lee Martin's cracking goal won it for us.

The win justified Ferguson's decision. You cannot dispute the fact that he did the best thing for Manchester United. It is as cut and dried as that. He put aside Jim's feelings even though they had known each other for about 15 years. If Les had conceded a soft goal, the Boss would have been crucified, so it was a massive gamble. Jim had made a few bad mistakes that season and the fans were edgy about him. The Press dwelt on this and Jim never regained his confidence. He came to Wembley with us, but it was hard to know what to say to him. We bought him a drink after the game, but he did not feel part of it. He and Alex knew that the decision had effectively marked the end of the road for him at United.

The 1990 FA Cup Final against Crystal Palace was one of contrasting fortunes for two goalkeepers. *Right:* Jim Leighton, with an understandably hang-dog expression, walks to his seat on the bench for the replay, while Alex Ferguson celebrates with Les Sealey, who kept a clean-sheet in the replay (*opposite below*). *Bottom:* We celebrate a well-earned triumph.

That FA Cup triumph came at a good time for the manager and the team. The new, and young, players must have wondered what they had walked into at first, and even the experienced pros, such as Webb and Phelan, had come from clubs that don't get the sort of stick we received. I'd known criticism at United before, but then it had been borne by senior pros, who were hardened to it. Yet the abuse we faced brought us together and the FA Cup was the ideal trophy to win, because of its charisma.

I would not class it as one of my finest seasons. It was interrupted by frustrating injuries and it took me until the end of the season to start playing well again. Injuries had disrupted the squad, and the Boss had spent much of the season trying to knit together a side while the club was in disarray. One reason we did better in the FA Cup than in the League was that the first Cup game came in January, by which time we had played together for a few months and were beginning to forge a team pattern. Once things started clicking, we visibly grew in confidence.

Fergie had earned the respect of the players. The pressure on him was intense, but he never took it out on us. We all had every reason to feel immensely proud of fighting back against such adversity — and answering our critics in the best possible fashion. Ferguson had embarked on the biggest spending spree in the history of English football but it was Lee Martin and Mark Robins — two youngsters who had cost nothing — who had played a major part in rescuing the club in that dramatic season.

GLORY IN EUROPE

The summer of 1990 had been disenchanting for me personally, as I had suffered the achilles tendon injury that had forced me out of the World Cup Finals. When I went to see a specialist in London, he said: 'Bryan, it could have gone in two weeks or two years — it is the result of a whole career's worth of wear and tear and knocks.' Those words made it even harder to accept than when I had actually been taken off during the match against Holland, because fate had been against me with my achilles going during the Finals.

After the operation, while I was in plaster, some people were trying to start scare stories about me quitting, but I was as determined as ever to get back and help United win more honours. The operation had left a six-inch scar up the sheath of my achilles tendon, and the doctors scraped away five blood clots! It flared up on my first run after the operation and I feared that a second op might be needed, but after a visit to Harley Street I was given some tablets and stretching exercises and they did the trick.

A right old hullabaloo

There were many hopeful omens for the new season and I was desperate to be back as quickly as possible. The players had demonstrated that they were beginning to understand each other's capabilities and we had an excellent pre-season programme. United also had a very useful new player. In June 1990 Denis Irwin was bought from Oldham. He'd been watched on a number of occasions, and had greatly impressed the Boss and all the scouts. I would say he was a snip at £650,000 — Denis puts in pinpoint crosses, has exceptional movement off the ball and was soon chosen to take dead-ball kicks in matches. On his debut, two goals came from his crosses.

In spite of our optimism, United's early League form was fairly disappointing. We lost at Sunderland, and were beaten 4-0 at Anfield. Then, late in September, Arsenal won 1-0 at Old Trafford in a bad-tempered game. The result has all but been forgotten, however, in the hullabaloo about the mass brawl that resulted in both clubs being docked points (Arsenal two, United one) by the FA, who also imposed heavy fines. Niggles happen all the time in professional football, and it's difficult to say why Irwin and Anders Limpar having a dig at each other should have suddenly exploded as it did — Nigel Winterburn probably shouldn't have got involved, but then it all got out of hand.

Lee Sharpe, whose brilliant performances in the 1990-91 season earned him the PFA 'Young Player of the Year' award, here loses his shinpad as he stretches to tackle Barcelona's Juan Goicoechea.

United never really managed to put together a sustained run of wins in the League that season. We were unbeaten in December — and our seven unbeaten games in January earned Alex Ferguson the Barclays 'Manager of the Month' award — but United's consistency was not maintained and in a bad patch, which lasted from 12th January to 23rd March, we went without a League win in eight games. There was a simple explanation for this: there were too many games in the League when, mentally, players had their thoughts on the Cup matches we were involved in and may have been hesitant in giving their all in League encounters.

Of all the competitions we were in, oddly enough, we were least assured in our defence of the FA Cup. We opened our campaign with a 2-1 win against Don Howe's QPR. I had quite a duel with Ray Wilkins, and Mark Hughes shot us ahead with an instinctive goal. Our character came to the fore when Rangers equalised. We weren't playing that well but we persevered to gain the win. In the fourth round, we beat Bolton 1-0. The goal was a cracker: Sharp crossed and 'Sparky' hit a clean, crisp volley with perfect accuracy. After the game, Nat Lofthouse said: 'In all my life I have never seen anybody hit the ball on the full volley like Mark Hughes.'

We went out of the FA Cup at Carrow Road, so often an unhappy hunting ground for United. Fergie had never won at Norwich and United hadn't beaten the Canaries in a knock-out competition since 1906. We had gone unbeaten in 21 previous League Cup, FA Cup and Cup Winners' Cup matches, but the club was unhappy that the game had been switched to Monday night because of BSkyB coverage. Swapping the times of games is a trend that players hate — we all prefer playing matches on a Saturday.

It's a real headache for the fans, as well. Travelling down to Norwich for an evening game means taking time off work. In the event, that night, we played a composed passing game, and caused them all sorts of problems, but Robert Fleck opened the scoring for them after 27 minutes. McClair equalised and then they brought on Ruel Fox, whose pace caused us trouble — Dale Gordon's winner directly resulted from his work. I had a chance to equalise, a header at the far post that I should have scored with, but I hit the woodwork. We should have got the equaliser, and had played well, but we had given away two bad goals.

Some of our best performances that season came in the Rumbelows League Cup. After knocking out Halifax, we avenged our defeat at Anfield by beating the champions 3-1 at Old Trafford. Mark Hughes tore into the Liverpool defence, leaving Glenn Hysen shell-shocked, and scored with a tremendous long-range drive. The form of Lee Sharpe was one of the main factors in that victory. We had needed somebody with a bit of pace for some time and Lee gave us the option of playing the ball into Sparky and utilising his strength or feeding it out to Sharpe and using his pace. We always knew he had ability and it came to the fore when we played Liverpool. Lee was up against a first-class full-back in Steve Nicol and he slaughtered him.

United have a proud history of buying Irish players. In June 1990 Cork-born Denis Irwin became United's 50th Irish signing. He is strong at overlapping runs and delivers a good cross (*top:* Denis challenges Arsenal's Alan Smith). Some of our finest displays in 1990-91 were in the League Cup, including our semi-final victories against Leeds United (*opposite:* Brian McClair tussles for the ball with Chris Fairclough).

The fans were elated by that win over Liverpool, but when we went to second-placed Arsenal we were even better, and produced one of the greatest performances of the decade. Just five weeks after the Gunners had won at Old Trafford in the League, we went through to the quarter-finals of the Rumbelows League Cup with a stunning 6-2 victory at Highbury — it was the Gunners' first defeat in 17 games that season and their heaviest home loss since the War.

United cut Arsenal to ribbons

We simply played to our full potential. Sharpe was preferred to Webb, and it was his inspired performance that tore Arsenal apart. Lee and Danny Wallace had a free role, and cut them to ribbons. Arsenal were square at the back and we had far too much pace for them. Our passing game was so accurate, imaginative and fast that the Arsenal defenders spent much of the game watching the ball as if it were a pinball. Ince and Phelan controlled Paul Davis and Michael Thomas in midfield. Altogether it was one of the best performances I have ever seen from a Manchester United team.

We took the lead through another of Clayton Blackmore's blistering free kicks after less than two minutes, and Sharpe scored his first hat-trick, including a marvellous curling shot from outside the box. Our wingers cut swathes through their full-backs time and time again, and, from one move by Wallace, Hughes received the ball in the heart of the box, and he dispatched it with aplomb. McClair and

Wallace got the other goals. After the game, Alex Ferguson told the Press: 'My players were totally magnificent. It was my biggest victory at United. I saved it for a special occasion.'

In the quarter-final, against Southampton at the Dell, we earned a replay with a late equaliser by Hughes. I headed a corner on and Sparky, who had been standing with his hands on his hips a split second before, reacted, adjusted and fired home a splendid volley. That gave us a replay and showed Mark's predatory instincts in an even clearer light. We won the replay 3-2, with a brilliant Hughes hat-trick. Jimmy Case was shown the red card, for a trip on me, by George Courtney. I was about 40 yards from goal when I was felled, so I had every sympathy for Jimmy. I thought the sending off was harsh — and the rule about players who are tripped while going for goal is a flawed one. I'd have been caught by the full-back coming over to cut me off. I said to Jimmy as he went off: 'There's nothing I can do.'

Sharpe was again in superb form when we defeated Leeds United 2-1 in the first leg of the semi-final. After the game Howard Wilkinson said the result would be good enough to secure their Wembley place. I never agree with managers who say that. If you are up against Liverpool, United, Arsenal or Leeds and go down by a goal, it is not a great result, because the top teams are always equipped to go

Top: **Ron Atkinson and Alex Ferguson lead out their teams for the 1991 League Cup Final.** *Opposite:* **Jim McGregor treats Les Sealey, after the 'keeper had gashed open his knee. Sealey, in his own unobtrusive way, had said that he was determined to carry on.**

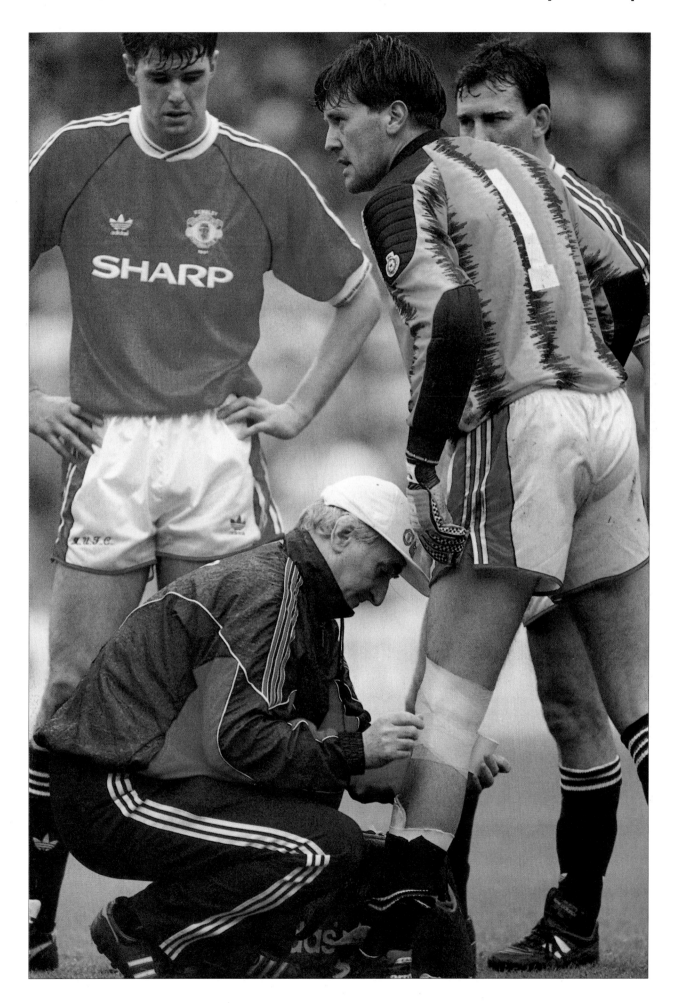

Above: **I'm keeping my eyes on the ball, while Montpellier's Carlos Valderamma looks on. He did not prove to be a potent opponent.** *Opposite:* **Paul Ince rides a challenge well in the same match.**

anywhere and win. That comment was a real hostage to fortune, since we beat them in the second leg.

We would have preferred to have had the home leg second, but we were in control of both games, made a lot of chances and worked very hard to get the result. The second leg came four days after our FA Cup defeat at Norwich and the whole team talk was about getting over the disappointment of that game — and using the match as a test of character.

When all your team perform as well as they possibly can, then you have a great chance of winning any semi-final. That's exactly what happened. We didn't try to protect our lead, although we did defend soundly when we had to, and Les Sealey performed magnificently in goal. Mal Donaghy replaced Steve Bruce, who was out with a toe injury, and he put in an excellent display. I was happy with my own display in midfield — I almost managed to score after 20 minutes when I got some power behind a header from Lee Sharpe's cross, but John Lukic saved — and Neil Webb was just great.

Our performance was of the highest quality, and it was matched by the only goal of the game, which was scored by Sharpe in the dying seconds of the match. McClair executed the perfect through ball and Sharpe rounded Lukic to fire in from a narrow angle. We had admirably retained our composure amid the ferocity of Elland Road. Lee was just so cool, especially when taking what was his sixth goal in the competition that season. The main thing, though, was that we went prepared to win.

The League Cup Final brought us face-to-face with Ron Atkinson and his impressive Sheffield Wednesday side. We had been beaten only once in

our previous 26 Cup matches, but we were painfully short of imagination and zest at Wembley. Our pre-match preparation was to run at them to see how they would take it, but we only managed this in little spells of pressure in the first half and that gave them time to settle. Unfortunately, too many of the players who had done so well in getting us to the Final just didn't play. Their goal came from a free kick clearance by Gary Pallister. The ball fell to John Sheridan and his shot flew into the net. We pushed forward more in the second half and our former 'keeper, Chris Turner, tipped a diving header from McClair over the bar with about eight minutes remaining. I was pleased that Ron had done such a tremendous job at Hillsborough. I wasn't pleased for him on that day, though.

So the League Cup went to a Second Division side for the first time in 16 years. People explained our defeat by saying that we took them too lightly, but having the semi-final of the Cup Winners' Cup the following week was the real problem. United tried to coast and win it without taking too much out of ourselves and our approach backfired. You can't do that in a Final. When we needed to step up a gear we couldn't. That said, I still felt we were the better team over 90 minutes and if the game had come at a different time we would have lifted the trophy.

Europe was the big challenge that season. We started our first European campaign for six seasons against the Hungarians Pecsi Munkas, and we couldn't have had easier opposition. In the first few games in Europe you just have to do a professional job and dispose of smaller opponents before facing a top club. Good goals from Blackmore and Webb earned a comfortable 2-0 victory. The result was more important than the performance. There was anxiety because of the lack of European experience and we possibly treated them with too much respect. In the away leg we finished them off thanks to a header from Brian McClair.

Wrexham, managed by Brian Flynn, are no mugs; just ask George Graham and the boys at Arsenal. Because they'd finished bottom of the Football League the previous season, everyone was writing it off as a no-contest, even though they had six seasons of European experience and had beaten FC Magdeburg, Hajduk Split and FC Porto during that

time. However, we were very aware that Brian had done an excellent job on a shoestring budget. The lads were disappointed to miss out on a glamorous tie, but the fans probably welcomed the chance to save a few quid in travelling expenses before the later rounds. There were plenty of laughs about not forgetting your passport and about UEFA's rule that teams had to go to the opposition's country at least 24 hours before a match, but there was no joking when we came to playing. Although we had avoided a top-class side, we were taking no chances about jeopardising our place in the last eight. Goals from Bruce, Pallister and McClair won us the home leg 3-0. In the match at the Racecourse Ground we won 2-0 with goals from Mark Robins, after a fine penetrating run by Ince through the penalty area, and Bruce.

The quarter-finals pitted us against Montpellier. It was a nice draw. They were third in the French

League, which was getting good publicity and it was appealing for our fans to go there. Montpellier were highly rated after having eliminated former European Champions PSV Eindhoven and Steaua Bucharest. We certainly didn't start slowly in the first leg and our best move was our opening one. Sharpe controlled a high pass perfectly, taking it on the run and then sending a low diagonal cross along the penalty area which McClair rifled home.

Yet in the seventh minute, it all went awry when Lee Martin, on his own, prodded the ball into his own net. We talked at half-time about the need for composure and making space for ourselves by spreading balls out wide, but we failed to do that. Lots of people wrote us off after this draw. The sign that told me not to worry was that their players were delighted they had got a draw at Old Trafford, and obviously thought they would win the home tie comfortably. We knew it would be easier playing away against Montpellier, because like most Continental teams they had come to Old Trafford to defend in numbers. We were accused of naïvety against their guile, but our failure to win had more to do with the simple fact that we did not play well.

It was a volatile atmosphere in the *Stade de la Mosson*. In the away game we were excellent. I thought I was unlucky to be booked by the Austrian referee for a fairly soft tackle on Patrick Colleter. In over a decade of European football I'd not been close to a yellow card, but now I was banned for the next leg. 'It was the most important game of my career,' said Alex Ferguson, 'I had to transmit my knowledge about patience.'

Montpellier, because they were at home, had to be more adventurous, which gave us space to get in behind them. We had the break we needed with Clayton Blackmore's goal — a 30-yard free-kick that was fumbled by their 'keeper, Claude Barrab — but from then on we took control and played like a top European side. We passed precisely and cut them up. The Boss had thought out our tactics carefully, playing McClair as a deep-lying inside forward, using Phelan on the right side of midfield and encouraging Sharpe to pull their defenders over to the wing on the left side. That kept us compact in the centre and gave us the pace to break. We started cautiously but after Bruce had confirmed our superiority by scoring from the spot, we finished rampant, heading for goal. I was satisfied with everything except my booking.

People had predicted that I would have a very tough game because I was up against their star player, the Colombian Carlos Valderamma, but he did not impress me very much. The former South American 'Player Of The Year' did show some nice touches on the ball, just as he had when I played against him for England, but he wasn't like the great world players I have had to compete against — Platini, Gullit, Zico — because even though they are superb they are also tireless workers. Valderrama was

Right: **Mark Hughes beats Barcelona's José Alexanco in the European Cup Winners' Cup Final. 'Sparky' is truly a player for the big game. His two goals in the Final won the trophy for United — and were a delight for him as they came against his former club.**

a stroller. I found him quite easy to mark. Even though he was skilful, he did not get on the ball enough to do us real damage, because he would not work hard enough. He did not make it difficult for me. He had accomplished a lot in South America, and maybe he had got to the stage in his career where he had achieved what he wanted to and did not feel he had to prove anything.

A night of European glory

Legia Warsaw in the semis looked like being a hard match but we were comprehensive winners. We dominated the away leg from start to finish. It was easy for me to commentate for ITV because United played so well and made it easy to be complimentary. It was a good performance, especially as there was no atmosphere there and it was a dreary day. The pitch was large and that suited us. We had watched a video of their games against Sampdoria, and realised that the Italians had lost the tie because of their negative approach in Warsaw, settling for a draw. Legia were stronger away, so we went to seal it in Poland.

Legia took the lead against the run of play, but we immediately responded to going behind, which is the hallmark of a good team. United knew they had to

step up the tempo and did it in style. Sharpe took full advantage of his superior speed to break down the left. His cross created confusion and McClair prodded the ball home. Two minutes before half-time, sweeper Mark Jozwiak was sent off for a professional foul on Sharpe. That was the killer blow as far as Warsaw were concerned. Our second was a great goal from Hughes, after a fine interception tackle from Donaghy. Hughes cut inside his marker and blasted a low shot inside the post. Mark had done an exceptional job holding the line. Finally, Bruce hooked the ball in after 67 minutes to give us a 3-1 win. I was back for the second leg and started the move down that ended with Sharpe rifling in an excellent shot. The Poles got a consolation goal, but the game was a bit of an anticlimax.

Although we faced Barcelona, one of Europe's great clubs, in the Final in Rotterdam, we weren't overawed by their record. It was my biggest game for Manchester United and a fabulous night. The fans turned out in great numbers and created a terrific atmosphere, which lifted the team. Barcelona had already knocked out Dynamo Kiev and Juventus and they showed in 1992, in winning the European Cup with the same players, what a good team they were.

I did my best to drive United forward in wave after wave of attacks and I floated in the cross for our first goal. The marking in their defence was poor, but Bruce got in a good header and Mark made sure the ball crossed the line. In the 75th minute, I saw that one of their lads was about to play the ball into midfield and I read where he was trying to put it, so I cut it out and played a first-time pass through to Mark. I thought he had taken it too wide but he unleashed a hell of a shot. I was delighted for him scoring against his old club. When we later joked about him taking the ball too wide, he gave a wry smile and said: 'I knew I wouldn't miss.' Bobby Charlton said: 'When Mark took the ball past the 'keeper for that second goal, I said to myself: "Just make sure and sidefoot it!" Of course, he didn't. I thought, "Oh, you clown!" When his shot hit the back of the net I just exploded.'

Michael Laudrup is a player I have always admired. He is so dangerous when he breaks through from midfield, but we stopped him getting into the game. Phelan covered Laudrup magnificently and did not allow him any space. McClair marked their Dutch sweeper, Ronald Koeman, and pressed him every time he got the ball. Brian did a fabulous job.

Barcelona came back into the match in the last 10 minutes and pulled a goal back, but Les Sealey was not 100 per cent fit and their goal has to be put down to him — he let Koeman's shot sneak under him. The shot that Clayton Blackmore cleared off the line was the result of a bad back pass from Bruce — so the two chances they had created were from our mistakes. We had dominated them, and thoroughly deserved our win. Our instincts for Cup football didn't let us down in the biggest game.

There was no faulting the Boss's tactical acumen and Alex joined Barcelona's manager, Johan Cruyff, as the only manager to win this trophy with two clubs. 'The last 10 minutes were like 10 years for me,' said Fergie. It was a proud night for me and I

Winning the Cup Winners' Cup was one of the real highlights of my United career. *Above:* I raise the trophy, while Brian McClair salutes our supporters.

rate is as one of my finest performances. We were all jubilant and had a great celebration, although Steve Bruce's comment to one reporter — which appeared in a paper the following day — that our dressing room was 'strangely quiet' after the game, must have been said with his tongue firmly in his cheek.

The one sad aspect of the season was that Rangers had lured Archie Knox to Ibrox. Archie had enjoyed his stay at United but the move was perfect for him and his family. He left behind a flourishing squad. Alex had tied up players on long-term contracts, and I also signed a further two-year contract at the end of the season. Despite the speculation, there had never been any real chance that I would be leaving. As the Boss put it: 'Bryan may not get you 15 goals a season now, but he has a lot of other qualities, not least his standing at the club as a leader. The players rightly respect him and I am looking to him as a captain to take us through the minefields involved in trying to win a title.' That European triumph had been the most satisfying night the club had had since 1968, but would it prove to be the springboard for even greater glory?

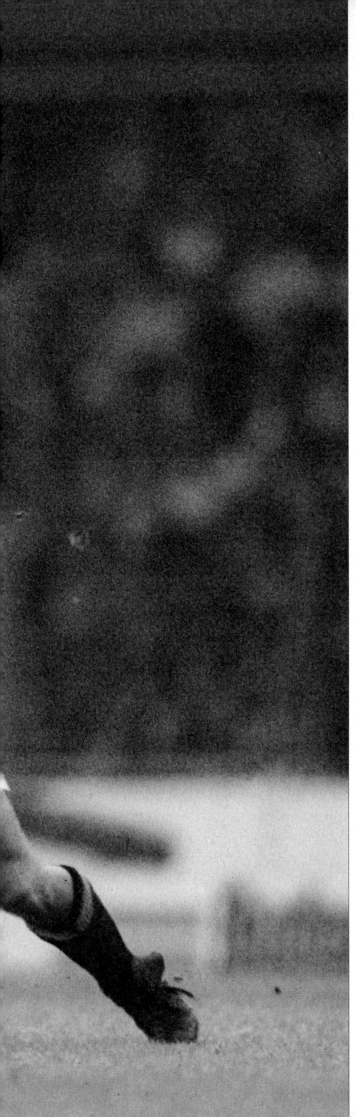

A TEAM OF TITANS

Building a winning team is what being a manager is all about. The Boss of Manchester United has one resource in this quest that is not available to many of his counterparts — money. Ron Atkinson spent more than £8 million in his reign, and Alex Ferguson doubled that expenditure in his first five years at Old Trafford.

The squad Ferguson inherited from Atkinson did not look likely to win the League. Ron recognised this himself. If he had stayed he would have built a new team around a few key players. Although Fergie did not even succeed to a team Ron was happy with, he gave us the chance to prove our worth, but after 18 months he decided that there was an unacceptable limit to what he could get from some of the squad.

The size of the task facing the new manager should not be underestimated, as he himself put it: 'When I arrived at United, and saw all the cracks, I said to myself: "Christ, this is a job and a half!" I even got to the point where I started doing diagrams, the structure of the club, the weaknesses on one side, the positive things on the other. Then, after a few days, I scrapped all that. It didn't work. The situation changed every day.' Alex knew that successful teams aren't created swiftly — but he also had a deep-seated ambition to rebuild on his own lines.

The gamble that paid off

Alex Ferguson's long-term transfer strategy was to reach the position — which he had achieved by 1992 — where he possessed a powerful, successful squad, that, if it needed replenishing, would require only a few players who could be introduced gradually. Hand-in-hand with that went a programme to rebuild entirely the club's youth structure.

To have any hopes of winning trophies a team can't give anything away at the back. That is the cornerstone of a sound team, because you can build an attacking strategy on that strength — as Alex himself had done at Aberdeen. When they were winning trophies regularly throughout the 1970s and 1980s, Liverpool never conceded easy goals.

Alex has done a good job tightening us up at the back. Steve Bruce has been a fantastic signing, a player of enormous heart. It is a pity that the nearest he has come to playing for England was when he captained the B team in Malta in 1986, because he is certainly one of the best defenders in Britain. A sturdy central defensive pairing is critical. Bruce and Paul McGrath looked great together, but as soon as

There is no holding down some players. Here, Ryan Giggs, who set the First Division alight in the 1991-92 season, gets away from some close marking. He is the most talented teenage player I have ever seen.

he lost McGrath the Boss knew he had to get Gary Pallister. Gary, who had been playing in the Second Division, hadn't proved himself at the top level, and the manager took a big risk in breaking the British transfer record to bring him to United. The gamble has paid off for both of them.

A manager must not be afraid of the obvious. In the English League a fair proportion of attacks come from high balls and you need someone who is good in the air, otherwise teams such as Wimbledon and Sheffield United will overwhelm you by continuously pumping the ball into your box. If there is no one who can clear it in the air then their forwards will knock the ball down into dangerous positions. Gary is great at combating an up-and-under team, but he also has skill on the ball, is quick and has grown in stature — his fellow pros recognised that in 1992 when they named him 'Player of the Year'.

The full-back positions took the manager time to sort out. Ferguson had doubts about John Sivebaek, and Mike Duxbury and Arthur Albiston were nearing the end of their United careers in Alex's early years, so his first signing was a full-back. Viv Anderson had already won a League medal with Nottingham Forest, and the manager thought this kind of experience was essential. I know that Viv himself is bitterly disappointed that injuries stopped him from ever showing his best form at United — something that also handicapped Colin Gibson.

Clayton Blackmore, Mal Donaghy, Paul Ince, Denis Irwin, Lee Martin, Paul Parker, Michael Phelan and Lee Sharpe have played at full-back since 1989, and although they have all done well, the manager would have preferred a settled pairing. Irwin and Parker offer a great hope for a solid partnership, but injuries meant they played together in only 25 out of 58 games in 1991-92.

Paul, who I rate as one of the best defenders in Europe, has brought a greater defensive awareness to our back four. There are times when his distribution could be better, but he does not give possession away very often. He has pace, strength and is explosively quick on the turn for recovery purposes. That's why he gets so many hamstring injuries. He gets tight on forwards and fights them with his body strength, which puts extra strain on the back of his legs. Paul missed 21 games in his first season here, all through hamstring injuries. Cork-born Denis Irwin is another excellent value-for-money signing. He is a brilliant dead-ball player and a fine defender; his impressive performances for United have helped him become a fixture in Jack Charlton's international plans.

The key area, of course, is the midfield — and Fergie rebuilt ours in 1989. I have enjoyed playing alongside Michael Phelan, Neil Webb and Paul Ince, although we fit together in different ways. Paul and I work as a pair — and that includes defending and building attacking moves. When United had Arnold Muhren and Steve Coppell in wide positions I got

Opposite: **Michael Phelan out-jumps Derby's Craig Ramage. Mike, who started as a central defender with Burnley, reads the game astutely and because of that he can do a sound job in a number of vital positions — throughout the midfield, or at full-back.**

forward all the time, because Steve worked hard at covering and Arnold rarely ventured into the opposition penalty area. I have heard people say that I'm not able to cover as much ground because I am slowing down; this is a factor, but the main reason I didn't hurtle into the opposition penalty area with such frequency in the 1991-92 season is because of the system we used. With two wide men, and Hughes and McClair in advanced positions, I could not afford to leave exploitable space behind me. When you have that system your central midfield players have to 'sit' more — holding a line in front of the defence to retain the shape of the team.

I like working very closely with my midfield colleagues. When tackling, I prefer a partner to stay close so he is there to have a second bite if I miss a challenge, or to collect the ball if I win it. You both have to be able to play on the ball, working little one-twos to break beyond the midfield without having to use your team-mates. That requires a good understanding. I had that with Ray Wilkins, and with Remi Moses, and I have it now with Phelan, Webb and Ince. When we play as a quartet, Mike, Paul and I hold the midfield line with Neil roaming free. With top players, you can improvise.

Paul Ince is a winner

Phelan is a player's pro, reliable and consistent, always working hard for the team. If he makes an error he never hides. Mike has great stamina, is able to play in several positions and reads the game well. His style didn't win over our fans at first, because a lot of his work is hidden. I like playing with Mike, because I know exactly what he is going to do. Those fans who interpret the game appreciate him. In the Cup Winners' Cup Final he did a magnificent job on the right side of midfield, which he doesn't particularly favour. He worked up and down all the game blotting Michael Laudrup out of the match. In the League Cup Final against Forest, he was played out of position but was probably our best player.

Neil Webb was bought for his creative abilities. He has the vision and passing range to prise open the opposition. Neil was very unfortunate with his achilles tendon injury, because it sapped his confidence and limited his mobility. He has really toiled to get fully fit again and has been unlucky to have missed out on important matches. That affected him as well, as he explained: 'The lowest point in my career was when I was left out of the Cup Winners' Final against Barcelona. That did not act as a gee-up. I was depressed and that terrible depression lasted quite a few months. I thought my career was destined to be elsewhere.' He stuck with it, though, and he has class — and class is something you need in a Manchester United team.

Paul Ince, who can dictate a game from in front of the back four, runs well with the ball and is a sharp, powerful ball-winner. Although he's not particularly good at opening up defences with through balls, his passes are constructive and tidy. People tag Incy as a controversial character, accusing him of chirping at referees all the time, but he is by no means the worst moaner I have ever heard on a football pitch. Paul has a great attitude to the game; he is a winner and one of the Boss's finest buys — not only for his talent, but for the fact that he is a bubbly personality in the dressing room.

Paul had a muted start at United, but he was having to adjust on and off the pitch. Fitting into a new team is never easy, and Paul was playing at right-back in a few of our games, which he was not accustomed to. In addition, living in a hotel didn't help him settle. I had a few chats to try and help him through a bad patch, as he later put it: 'Robbo got me through a crisis which could easily have led to a real bust-up with the manager. If I had expected sympathy from Bryan, I was badly mistaken. He gave me a real ticking off when I went to see him after I had been dropped. He told me to get grafting, that I was not giving enough of myself and that I was the only one who could prove myself. Robbo has every player's respect and I could take that kind of thing from him — and he was right!' Paul was only 22 when he arrived and had some maturing to do, but he has buckled down marvellously. It would be really pleasing to see him turn his undoubted scoring potential into goals. He could easily be getting into double-figures every season.

That would complement our front men, who are not deployed as an out-an-out striking partnership. It suits Brian McClair to play a withdrawn role, but frequently turning up in the box at the right time in the right position. He has a great instinct for goal, and the perfect attitude for a striker; if he misses a chance, he just shuts negative thoughts out. 'Choccy' was an inspired buy — he missed only three games out of 261 during his first five seasons, and bagged 102 goals. He works hard tracking people down and his strong running pulls opponents out of position.

Because Brian plays in a deep role, Mark Hughes, who was brought back to United in 1988 by Ferguson, often leads the line on his own. Mark excels in this role. His strength makes him really hard to dispossess, but he has wonderful touch for a power player. Forwards like Mark must have great skill because they are usually facing the wrong way when the ball comes to them. They have to be able to resist a challenge from behind, keep a pass under control and lay it off accurately — and 'Sparky' is a master at this. He runs opponents ragged, and frightens them because he can do the unexpected.

Below: **Danny Wallace prepares to take the ball outside Richard Shaw, the Crystal Palace left-back, in the 1990 FA Cup Final. Wallace is a talented player, but his United career has been blighted by injuries.** *Opposite:* **Paul Parker, warming up for Matt Busby's testimonial in August 1991, is one of the best defenders in Europe and strengthened our defence.**

But players respect him — that's why he won 'Player of the Year' twice in three years. The one area he can improve is his scoring rate. He grabs spectacular goals, but does not get his fair share of tap-ins, and that is because he does not anticipate where the bounces and ricochets fall. If he gets that into his game then instead of scoring 15 goals a season, he will be in the high 20s. Mark knows that himself.

Ferguson has also been able to get the best out of foreign players. He was tipped off about Andrei Kanchelskis by a Norwegian advertising agent who was doing some work for the club. Andrei found the English game hard to get to grips with, particularly the fact that the ball was in the air so much of the time, but he gave a host of sensational displays in his first season. He was only 22 when he arrived, and had a great deal to contend with: learning a new language, settling into a completely different way of life — and, to cap it all, he had just got married. We will not see the best of him for a couple of years — a frightening prospect for United's rivals! By then, he will have experience under his belt, his fitness will be sharper and his knowledge of the game broader. He was a remarkable steal by the Boss.

In the end, a Continental player was the answer to the club's goalkeeping problems. Jim Leighton started off well, but lost his confidence. In one match against Wimbledon he had his teeth knocked out in a fierce challenge. They set out to intimidate him and that's what they did. Jim lost a lot of conviction that day and he never really came back from it. Being dropped for the FA Cup Final replay, and playing in the reserves throughout the 1990-91 season, was demoralising and we were all pleased when he got the chance to rebuild his career at Dundee. Although Les Sealey did a great job he was not the long-term answer — that was Denmark's Peter Schmeichel.

Peter is in complete charge of his penalty area, because he has assured handling, appreciates angles and distributes well. His throw-outs are a valuable source of attacks. His presence is inspiring and he's brave and agile for a big man. Peter is sometimes a bit rash in coming for crosses he has not judged properly, but when he improves on that he'll be out on his own as the world's number one. In his first few games he was rattled by strikers jostling him as he went for catches. He said: 'Goalies aren't touched when we go for crosses in Denmark!' — so we gave him a lot of robust challenges in training and has learned to cope with the physical side of the game.

Although Alex has spent a lot of money, he is not just a cheque-book manager, as some critics have jibed. Spending lavishly does not in itself guarantee success — Everton have splashed out millions since 1989 and won nothing — you have to get the whole framework of a club right. Our Boss has rebuilt the youth system and nurtured two fantastic teenagers to international level. He knows that a mixture of youth and experience is the ideal blend. You need the freshness of lads who will do a lot of running, and

you have to have experienced lads who will slow youngsters down a bit and take responsibility for changing the pace of game when that is needed.

The club is protective about youngsters but that is vital at United. Once a kid is in the first team, promotional things are pushed his way and some people try to take advantage. I have done my best to advise Ryan Giggs and Lee Sharpe, the pick of the youngsters, occasionally saying: 'You shouldn't do that!', but whether they act on advice is down to them. Sometimes lads will accept guidance more easily from a player than a manager — it might seem as though the Boss is just getting at them, but it's best done in a low-key way. Ryan and Lee show respect, and come to me for help sometimes. They are young and they will get high spirited now and

Right: **Peter Schmeichel, our superb Danish goalkeeper, makes a one-handed save in the Rumbelows Cup semi-final second leg at Old Trafford, pushing the ball away from Middlesbrough's Paul Wilkinson.**

again. They might do something which is a bit over the top, but then they'll get a rap over the knuckles for it, and will learn the hard way! I have no doubt they'll come through, as they are both sensible lads.

In that 1990-91 season Lee turned the key for United. His pace tears up defences. He created a tremendous stir and Ryan had a similar brilliant impact a season later. Giggs is set to be one of United's all-time greats. Technique in itself is as boring in football as in anything else, and players like Giggs add that vital element of artistry to a team. His skill, even though he's a boy, is sublime.

The character of a player is very important to Ferguson. He doesn't like what he calls 'no triers', he wants winners — players who will go through the pain barrier for Manchester United, people who can

get success, handle it and build on it, demanding more of themselves. He looks at a player's character as closely as their playing ability. He's invariably spot on with his assessment of a player, but you can't guarantee that things will always turn out right. Temperament can't be measured at a fitness test. The hottest properties on the training ground can freeze in a match. Yet of the 22 players he signed in his first five years only a couple failed to fulfil their potential.

Great things were expected of Danny Wallace, but he has been very unfortunate with injuries. While he has been out, other players have come through and established themselves, so whenever he has returned he has had to make an impact straight away. Danny lost a stone in weight for the start of the 1990-91 season, and just as he had recaptured his form — he

THE MAGIC OF RYAN

Everyone in the game has been impressed by Ryan Giggs. Terry Yorath, the Wales manager, made him the youngest player ever to represent his country as a full international — and he was voted PFA 'Young Player of the Year' in his first full season. From the moment Ryan started training with the first team, it became obvious that he is an exceptional player.

Ryan was United daft as a youngster, but by a quirk of fate he was enrolled in Manchester City's School of Excellence when he was 13. The forms stipulated that no other club could get him for at least a year, so it was a quite a tense time for Alex Ferguson, who had been tipped off about Giggs by Harold Wood, a long-serving United ground steward. 'When Bobby Charlton saw Ryan score six goals in a boys' match not long after he'd arrived at Old Trafford,' said Fergie, 'Bobby gave me a look and said: "Thank God we got him."'

Ryan has two marvellous feet and his control is perfect. His vision is great and he can finish well — he scored seven goals in his first season, some of them with exceptional strikes. But if there is one thing that separates him from other promising youngsters and gives him a real chance of being an all-time great, it is his balance. It is glorious. Ryan's ability to control a fast-moving ball is due to his incredible balance — and he has a body swerve that wrong-foots opponents at will. In addition, he has a good temperament. He played 51 games in 1991-92, ending up with a League Cup medal. It is an achievement in itself for a boy of his age to hold down a place over the whole of his first season, but Ryan was consistently brilliant.

The Boss himself said: 'Just when you think a tackler is going to get a foot to a ball, Giggs seems to float or roll over a challenge. The defender always seems to go down while the boy stays on his feet. And he has the bottle to go on doing that under pressure. He's got those eyes, the kind that look right through you, cold as steel. Like all young players he's going to have to put up with older hard cases saying: "Stay away from me, son, if you know what's good for you!" But I'm certain it won't work with him. He's a lovely lad, but there's not an opponent in football who will intimidate him.'

I told him to expect opponents to try and frighten him, but he rides tackles well. He is a lean lad, but he reads the game well and anticipates the timing and height of challenges and skips out of trouble. In some games in his first season you could see his concentration wondering when he had not been seeing much of the ball, but he is still learning the game. It will take a few years of playing football at the top level for him to get wise to the tricks of concentrating through different stages of a match. He will master that, because he wants to learn and wants to be a better player.

The Press dubbed him 'the new George Best', but that has happened to a lot of bright kids at United, some of whom have been no where near Besty's league. But in all the time I have been at Manchester United Ryan is the only one I would have said that about.

was superb when we beat Arsenal 6-2 in the League Cup — he was hit again by injury problems and was not able to win back a place.

The transition between a small club and Old Trafford can overawe players. Alex brought in a number of players who had been the stars at their former clubs, and they had to adjust to being just another face in a squad of celebrated international players. Nobody should underestimate the size of the problem for players coming from small clubs to United, where you are plunged from playing one big game in every six to a big game every week.

Alex signed a lot of highly gifted players — and great players can need *more* managing. Highly talented players can be eccentric in lifestyles and strong-minded. They usually have their own opinions on how football should be played, know the way they want to play and may be reluctant to change that for anybody. If you can harness the talents of exceptional players and good pros, and knit them into a cohesive team, then you are on the road to victory.

To achieve success in the game now you need a large squad — the sheer volume of matches is daunting. United will finish the 1992-1993 season having competed in the Premier League, the FA Cup, the League Cup and the UEFA Cup, involving up to 70 games. Ferguson has deliberately created a strong pool because the more successful you are, the greater the need for strength in depth. When everyone is fit you get a bit of unrest from the people who are left out, but that is only natural, particularly as there are nearly nine internationals on the sidelines in any one week at United! The manager has to motivate them so they still feel part of it. Having such a depth of talent creates another problem for a manager — what is his best team? For Alex this has been a real problem, because there is not much to choose between certain top players.

Having a surplus of players hungry to win a place is a complication that any manger would prefer to a mediocre squad — and there is no doubt that the squad for 1992-93 is the best of my United career. From 1989 to 1992 the team was still at a developing stage. Alex bought the right players but it took time for them to fuse into a confident and assured team. We were capable of winning cups, but it takes a well-rooted team to produce the kind of consistency that wins the title. Ferguson has the vision to build a championship side because he knows the blend that is required. Our task is to turn talent into titles.

Although Alex Ferguson has spent £16 million on constructing this squad, his transfer record stands up to scrutiny. His team has made the club successful and profitable. The quality of his buys will become even more clear in the years leading to the 1994 World Cup as a few more of his signings develop into established internationals — something I hope to see with Ince, Sharpe and Pallister. That will prove that even the international managers know that Ferguson has got the top players in the country at his club.

Opposite: **Andrei Kanchelskis, our superb flying winger, in action against Liverpool in the 0-0 draw in October 1991. Andrei had a sparkling first season.**

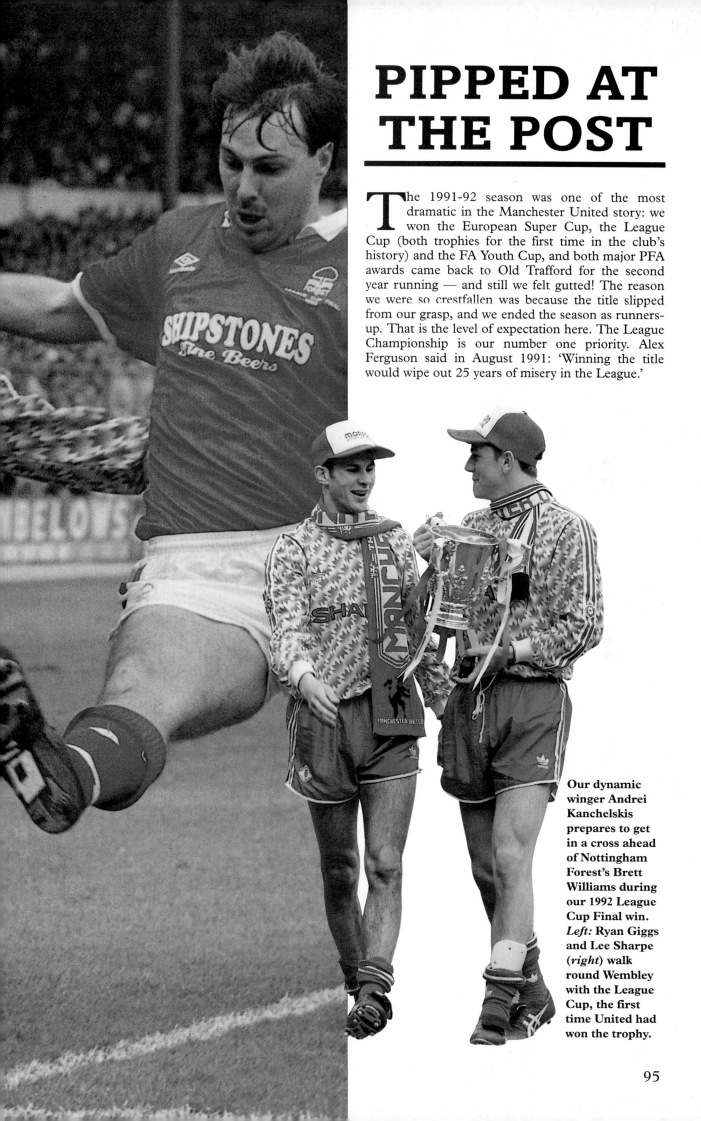

PIPPED AT THE POST

The 1991-92 season was one of the most dramatic in the Manchester United story: we won the European Super Cup, the League Cup (both trophies for the first time in the club's history) and the FA Youth Cup, and both major PFA awards came back to Old Trafford for the second year running — and still we felt gutted! The reason we were so crestfallen was because the title slipped from our grasp, and we ended the season as runners-up. That is the level of expectation here. The League Championship is our number one priority. Alex Ferguson said in August 1991: 'Winning the title would wipe out 25 years of misery in the League.'

Our dynamic winger Andrei Kanchelskis prepares to get in a cross ahead of Nottingham Forest's Brett Williams during our 1992 League Cup Final win. *Left:* **Ryan Giggs and Lee Sharpe (*right*) walk round Wembley with the League Cup, the first time United had won the trophy.**

I had really thought that 1992 would be the year that the championship came back to Old Trafford — and I was amazed that the bookies had United at 12-1 for the title. I could not contemplate that with the squad we possessed we could possibly end out of the top three. The squad had been together for three years, had grown in confidence after winning the Cup Winners' Cup and was crammed with talent: we had 15 internationals, with nearly 400 caps between us. Three of the internationals — Peter Schmeichel, Paul Parker and Andrei Kanchelskis — were new signings, and they were three superb buys. We had a successful pre-season tour of Norway and Scotland, and I was fit for the first game of the season, which made a welcome change!

One of our ambitions was to become the first team to defend the Cup Winners' Cup, but this quest ended in the autumn. We had not looked convincing in our first game, against Athinaikos. Their pitch was full of ruts, making it impossible to play passing football, and the temperature was too hot to handle; I was roasting and I was just watching — and we had to be satisfied with a 0-0 draw. The drawbacks of European football were plain to see: a lengthy delay

at the airport, followed by a tiring flight, left only two days to recover for the next game. Two weeks later the return leg went to extra time, but Hughes and McClair broke the deadlock to pull us back from the brink of a European disaster.

In the next round we lost 3-0 at Atletico Madrid. Against teams like Atletico, in their own stadiums, you can't have a bad period of the game or you'll be punished — and that is what happened. Over 88 minutes, during which they led by a breakaway goal, we were the dominant team, but in the last two minutes we conceded two goals, which effectively put us out of the Cup. It was naivety, but we learned the hard way. Although we got off to a good start in the second leg, when Hughes scored with a header in the fourth minute, we could not maintain the pace and it ended 1-1. Atletico deserved to go through, but we

Below: **Peter Schmeichel celebrates Steve Bruces's winner against Ron Atkinson's Aston Villa in August 1991. It was United's first win at Villa Park under Alex Ferguson.** *Opposite:* **Neil Webb and Paul Parker (***centre***) both struggle to take the ball away from Carlton Fairweather in our 2-1 win at Wimbledon.**

preserved one distinguished record: United have not lost at home in 49 European ties in over 35 years.

Our main aim was the League Championship — and our first game, home to Notts County, was in front of 46,278 fans, with thousands more locked outside. Kanchelskis and Parker had great debuts and I managed to score with a pleasing long-range volley. On the last day of August we faced our first major test — Leeds United. Howard Wilkinson had spent millions during the summer, on Tony Dorigo, Rod and Ray Wallace and Steve Hodge. We were trailing 1-0 with five minutes left, but I fired home an equaliser. We gave them a goal start, when Peter Schmeichel misjudged the flight of a cross, giving Lee Chapman a free header, but we created dozens of chances and deserved to win. We played at a ferocious pace, in the hottest playing conditions I have ever experienced in Britain. David Batty later told me that their players had been astonished by our work-rate. We had our best start to a season under Ferguson, and the Boss won Barclays 'Manager of the Month' award for August. In that period we also took heart from the way that Liverpool and Arsenal, who I expected to be our real rivals, were slipping up.

On 28th September we met second-placed Spurs, and played top-class football, controlling the tempo of the game and carving out chances. I had a hand in our first goal and scored an 86th minute winner with a header. The Boss said: 'What a splendid example at 34 Bryan continues to set. Players of 24 must say to themselves: "If he can do it, so can I!" He benefitted from having a complete break this summer. He is

lovely and fresh and everyone is responding.' It had been a wonderful month. United had won all five League matches, including a fine display to hammer Luton 5-0, and beaten Cambridge in the League Cup.

October, however, was a muted contrast. We had some big games to play but failed to maintain our momentum. We missed a real chance to sprint ahead by drawing at home with Arsenal and Liverpool, when we created enough chances to have won them both easily. In the last League game of the month — the unlucky 13th match of the campaign — just days after our defeat in Spain, we lost 3-2 at Sheffield Wednesday, our first defeat of the season. We cruised through the first half and went in 2-1 up at the break, but tiredness suddenly caught up with us and we faded badly in the closing stages of the match.

November was a far more encouraging month. We captured some silverware by winning the European Super Cup against Red Star Belgrade, with a 67th minute winner from McClair. In fairness, Red Star, who had won the Champions' Cup against Marseille, were the better side. They were full of brilliant technicians and had some spellbinding attacks.

Giggs — the poker-faced genius

United showed artistry of our own in an absolute purple patch in which we played the best football of any League team that season. We possessed complete attacking conviction: we went out to win in style. In the first game of this run we beat West Ham 2-1, with goals from Ryan Giggs and myself. Ryan was mesmerising, and he scored with a superb volley. He met McClair's cross on the full as he was racing into the box and gave the ball a deadly bit of swerve that made it fly into the corner of the net. His poker-face expression as he bears down on goal frightens the life out of some defenders.

Our beautiful, one-touch, passing football was at the core of our 3-1 victory at Crystal Palace the following week. Although we went a goal behind, we kept our shape and self-belief. The Boss was bold, persisting with Kanchelskis and Giggs on the flanks, with Webb and myself in the middle, and we severed the Palace formation. Our defence was rock solid, our midfield mobile, there was intelligent movement from McClair and Hughes and our wingers were so quick-witted that they were impossible to shut down. United were made 6-5 favourites for the title.

We followed that with a League Cup win over Oldham, we also beat Coventry 4-0, Chelsea 3-1 and, on Boxing Day, stuffed Oldham 6-3, a game in which Andrei scored a wonder goal. He swept in from the right, beat two defenders and took the ball wide of the goal, then checked back and shot past the 'keeper and the despairing lunge of Earl Barrett. The only drawback was that I took a knock on my recently-injured calf muscle, which meant I'd miss the games at Leeds. Oldham's Boss, Joe Royle, said: 'It is never easy when 11 internationals catch fire. United have a higher capability than anyone else.'

We were buzzing with confidence at that stage of the season — relishing every game. In all the time I have been at United, the team has usually gone through a lean patch from late November up to the New Year, but after that defeat at Hillsborough we remained unbeaten for the remainder of 1991. We were dominating games to a degree where opponents were hardly given a glimpse of our goal, and because our confidence was sky-high we were a daredevil attacking force. At that time, no one here would have thought it possible that we could go into a decline.

One of the factors in the change was the Leeds United trilogy. On 29th December we went to Elland Road for a vital League clash. Webb scored a neat

Left: **After surging past Martin Keown, Andrei Kanchelskis slips the ball past Neville Southall in United's 1-0 defeat of Everton in January 1992.**

A GOLDEN OPPORTUNITY

Michael Phelan (right), in an interview for this book, said: 'Alex Ferguson gave a lot of players the chance to play for United and there is no question about it — he had our complete loyalty in that difficult 1989-90 season, and our confidence grew steadily after that FA Cup win. We set out to make progress from that win and we achieved that. Alex is a thoughtful man, totally dedicated to the team, and he has helped me cope with things.

The Boss has strengthened the squad to the position where there are likely to be over half a dozen internationals left out. It is very hard to bide your time in the reserves, and the wait is longer when things are going well, but the manager wants players who will respond with the right attitude and work even harder to stake their claim. That breeds success. Alex picks the team he thinks will win.

My versatility has been both an asset and a handicap. The advantage is that I am favoured to do certain jobs such as man-to-man marking roles — for example when I marked Michael Laudrup in the Cup Winners' Cup Final — but the drawback of being able to do a specific job in a foreign position is that you don't establish a set role, although in the 1991-92 season I had been a regular until my injury.

United were very convincing in 1991-92, but all of us agreed that our success had been punished with a fixture pile-up at the end. I don't begrudge Leeds their title, because they are a fine side, but we handed it to them. Those last four weeks proved too hard to handle for us. I don't think we dealt with the intensity of our fans desire for that trophy. I had been in that position once before, in the 1988-89 season, with Norwich. We had been top or second for the first eight months, but our confidence snapped in the final run-in and we finished fourth. At Carrow Road, though, they still celebrated, because it was their highest position ever, but at Old Trafford we were all just shell-shocked, totally dismayed. We knew we had thrown away a golden opportunity.

I think the Easter League game against Nottingham Forest was the turning-point, because we played really well that day but lost 2-1. Our next game was at West Ham. We were tense and were not helped by the aggressive atmosphere generated by their fans.

We didn't function at all that night and could have done with Robbo. He is so vastly experienced that you can't help but be influenced by his attitude. He is a winner in everything he does. I have seen opponents put off by his sheer presence. We did miss him at the

run-in — any team would miss a player of his class — but we had been playing well without him and Bryan, being the inspirational captain he is, made his contribution from off the field. We have a sound team, which has won three trophies, and that title failure may be the final building block in our make-up. We have the character to come back from it. We all want to see Robbo with a championship medal.'

---

volley, but Leeds forced a draw. We were the better team but sat back when we should have finished them off. We conceded a bad penalty and were punished. Even so, we were satisfied as 1991 ended. We'd come through a hard period with good results.

The first setback was certainly dramatic — a 4-1 drubbing by QPR at Old Trafford on New Year's Day. All our players had an off-day and the Boss was certainly unimpressed: 'I have never had a team who on the day were such an abject failure,' he said. The rumour factories went straight into overdrive, with reports that the players had been out on a New Year's Eve rave-up, but we had followed our usual practice of spending the Christmas period in a hotel. Players are far too professional to drink before a big

Opposite: Ryan Giggs demonstrates his poise and balance as he begins a run against the Leeds United defence in our 1-1 draw in August 1991.

game. The defeat was simply the result of a dire performance from us, and a good one from QPR.

The team were keen to make immediate amends, which they did with a magnificent 3-1 win at Leeds United in the Rumbelows Cup. I was missing for that game, but played in the reserves at home to Bolton on 13th January. I scored in a 1-1 draw and reflected on the strength in depth we had: that reserve team contained six internationals: myself, Phelan, Donaghy, Wallace, Sharpe and Irwin — and we also had Walsh, Martin and Robins.

The third part of the Leeds trilogy was an FA Cup tie. We demonstrated how to handle pressure. I was a substitute that day and although Leeds had the better of the play, we showed our cutting edge just before half-time. McClair robbed Hodge and fed a superb reverse ball to Giggs, who raced down the line. Ryan looked to have taken the ball a step too far but he sent over an inch-perfect cross that evaded two Leeds defenders and was met by Hughes, who nodded it firmly into the net to give us a victory.

Our FA Cup progress was shortlived. We drew 0-0 at the Dell, and then made a fantastic come-back in the replay, from two-goals down, to level and take the match with Southampton into extra time. My 'goal', a header that crossed the line, was not given, and the game went into a penalty shoot-out. We had drawn up a list of takers — with Webb, Irwin, McClair, Ince and myself — but I had strained my calf muscle, so the Boss asked the lads who would take one, and Giggs answered the call. Giggs and Webb, who took the first penalty, both missed, and United picked up a unenviable record — the first Division One side to go out of the FA Cup in a penalty shoot-out. Before any future Cup replay we'll have our shoot-out routine running like clockwork.

The replay, and the gruelling extra time, did not help us in our League campaign. In February and March United were showing signs of fatigue and we weren't getting particularly good results, winning only one of six games in February. We had stopped playing attractive football and were anxious. We kept playing the ball forward too early, which made it hard for Hughes and McClair to get on top of their markers. A passing and moving game had been the source of our early success and when our passing football waned, we stuttered, dropping points against Notts County, Chelsea, Arsenal, Coventry and Sheffield Wednesday. Some of the goals we conceded in this period were sloppy, a result of loss of concentration.

This sequence shows my 'goal' in the FA Cup fourth round replay at home to Southampton. *Below:* I get in-between their defenders to head the ball. *Opposite below:* I raise my arm to claim the goal. The ball definitely went completely over the line — the *Daily Star*, whose photographer was on the side, level with the goal-line, sent me a picture of the goal. I reacted quite strongly, because although the referee's view may have been obscured, the linesman was right in line with the action and should have signalled for a goal. That would have given us a 3-2 lead, but the tie went to a penalty shoot-out, which we lost.

Knocking Leeds out of the Cups, and drawing with them in a hard League game, took more out of us than we'd at first realised. During those late winter and early spring weeks, we were still in the two Cup competitions, playing frequently, but our rhythm went and, more damagingly, we stopped scoring. The Old Trafford pitch was also working against us. It had come out of the winter months in bad shape, turning into a mud bath when wet, and a rutted, sand-filled obstacle course when dry. This hampered our attempts to keep playing fluent, passing football, and we were also hit by a few niggly injuries, so when people came back after a few games out they were not firing on all cylinders. This dip in form hit Giggs and, in particular, Kanchelskis. In early March Andrei went to Fergie and said he thought he needed a rest. The Boss had noticed, of course — Andrei had been taken off six times in a matter of two months. This was the moment in the season when we should have built a massive gap between us and Leeds United.

We were still capable of excellent performances, and none better than when we beat Sheffield United 2-1 at Bramall Lane in March. We had won a place in the League Cup Final and were boosted by the return of Sharpe. It was our fourth win in 10 games in 1992, and we were masterful. Even though we fell behind, we played cool, incisive football, slowly unravelling the Sheffield defence. The Boss seemed happy: 'It's the best day since I got married,' he said.

That win did not spark us back into form, though. We lost at Nottingham Forest — our second defeat in 29 games — and then had a dreadful goalless draw with Wimbledon. By this time the Old Trafford pitch was so full of sand that one player joked: 'Someone will come out with deckchairs at half-time!' We all knew that it was no longer a question of ability. It was purely and simply a war of nerves between us and Leeds. Our fans are nearly always a great asset, but occasionally we can get caught up in their mood. Leeds had thrashed Wimbledon 5-1 a week before and the crowd expected us to tear them apart. If the game goes for a long period without a goal, the fans' frustration passes on to the pitch. The players stop playing patiently, which is counterproductive against

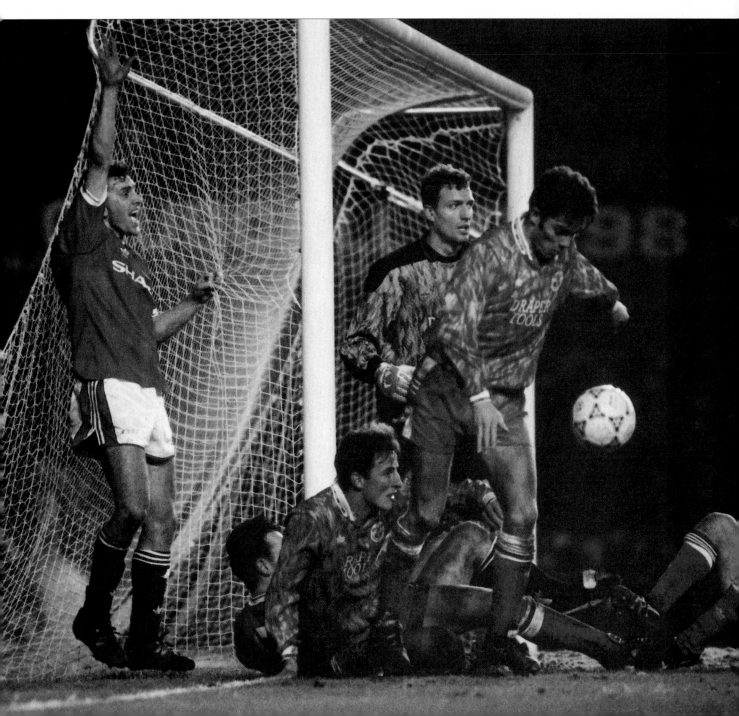

a team (as Wimbledon did) that is just sitting back. I can sympathise with the fans, though, as I spent the game as a spectator, willing the ball into the net.

I then spent an agonising week waiting to see if there was any improvement in my calf muscle injury. On the morning of our game at QPR, I went for a trial run in Hyde Park. Ince was suspended and Blackmore injured, and we needed another midfield player, so I decided to play even though I had not trained for a fortnight. Alex Ferguson told the Press: 'Once Robbo told me he was fit, there was no way I could leave him out. He went through pain to play.' I was given the job of breaking up their attacks, and holding our midfield. As we sat in the dressing room, we heard the loud, inspirational chant of our fans — 'Ferguson's Red and White Army' — ringing round Loftus Road. QPR, who'd lost once in 18 games, made it hard for us, and although a 0-0 draw was not a terrible result, we created chances to win the game.

'We needed Robbo's experience'

On 31st March, at Norwich, United looked like true title contenders. McClair grabbed one goal and Ince scored two exceptional goals. We joked afterwards that for once United would be glad to pay the £5000 fee West Ham get when 'Incy' turns out for us. I had been surprised at how well the QPR match had gone for me, but my calf injury was obviously severe, because I limped off with a recurrence of it. I wasn't totally depressed, because of the fine display we had given. It was full of the sort of inventive, flowing attacks that we had been producing week-in-week-out only three months before. When we came away from Carrow Road, I thought: 'That's it! We'll go from strength to strength from here.' Our optimism seemed well-founded, because, on 4th April, Manchester City beat Leeds 4-1 at Maine Road, which left us top by a point with two games in hand.

Three days later City were the visitors to Old Trafford. This was the one game of the campaign when we showed real inexperience — when mentally we defeated ourselves. Giggs scored a dazzling goal and I couldn't see City scoring. Then, when Neil Pointon was sent off and tempers flared on both sides, we allowed ourselves to become distracted — and let City get some passion into their play. Bruce, with his normal cool head, would never have conceded such a reckless penalty, but he was still fuming about the tackle on Giggs. Ferguson later said: 'It was when City had their man sent off that we really needed Robbo's experience. He would have settled us down and kept us calm and there is no doubt we would have won.'

Five days later, playing with complete composure, United won the League Cup. It was disappointing to miss out on a Final, but I had played a solid part in our road to Wembley. Our path to the Final in 1991 had been extraordinarily hard and it had been pretty tough to get there in 1992. Our first three opponents — Cambridge United, Portsmouth and Oldham — were all tricky, but the quarter-final at Leeds was the hardest game. There was a red-hot atmosphere at Elland Road, and we knew it was the sort of game where you thrive or disappear, but my team-mates played with self-belief and style.

Speed put Leeds ahead, but we levelled through a breathtaking Clayton Blackmore free kick. After Dorigo went off injured, we exploited their lack of shape and tied them in knots. A heavy responsibility had fallen on Giggs's shoulders, because the service to Kanchelskis had been cut off, but Ryan, who netted one himself, split Leeds with a brilliant through ball and Kanchelskis beat the advancing John Lukic. Wilkinson said: 'They deserved their win. They were quicker, sharper and hungrier than us, and did what was necessary to create and hold a lead.' Leeds had previously lost once in 28 games.

Middlesbrough, our opponents in the semi-final, were no walkover. The first leg at Ayresome Park, which ended 0-0, was a fair result and Steve Pears, a former United 'keeper, made some great saves. In the second leg, a week later, the pitch was sodden and muddy and the quality of our build-up play was superb considering the conditions. The ball was transferred swiftly between Ince, myself, Giggs and McClair before being passed to Sharpe, who hit a low screaming drive into the corner.

We thought that 'Boro would put most of their men behind the ball — which would have made it really hard because of the state of the pitch — but, all credit to them, they attacked and made it an open, exciting game. Five minutes into the second half they equalised and we had a real scrap on our hands. Pallister cleared off the line and, in extra time, Schmeichel flung himself to his left to claw out Willie Falconer's header from under the bar. It was a save worthy of winning any game. Even so, I believed we were going to go through. I got my head to a corner, the ball reached Giggs, and he scored a magnificent volley. The icing on the cake was the news that Leeds had been beaten 4-1 at QPR.

A damaging fixture pile-up

I had a blood clot on my calf muscle, and although I had intensive treatment, I could not be risked for the Final. It was a happy game to watch, though. United gave a first-class display, taking a grip on the match from the kickoff. We never looked like surrendering the initiative once McClair scored. Our midfield denied Forest any attacking options — Paul Ince and Mike Phelan gave quality displays. Alex Ferguson chose Phelan ahead of Webb because of the possible danger from Roy Keane and Nigel Clough. Fergie said: 'I thought Mike did a great job. Overall, I thought our midfield was stronger. They showed great patience, and from that springboard came our success.' Only a diving goalline clearance from Laws denied McClair a second after a perfect lay off from Hughes. We were all proud to have won the League Cup for the first time in the club's history.

Opposite: **Paul Ince, in the League Cup Final, acrobatically controls the ball at the shoulder of Forest's Scot Gemmill, while Mark Hughes looks on.**

That left a League run-in that was frighteningly intense: six games in 11 days! In the first of these, four days after the Final, we beat Southampton 1-0 with a superb volley from Kanchelskis. Southampton came for the draw and defended with nine men. They also tackled aggressively, and one challenge did great damage to our title hopes. Ince left Old Trafford on crutches because of damaged ankle ligaments following a crunching tackle.

People have said that my absence undid United, but myself *and* Ince being out of the team at the same time was the real stumbling block. United can cope with one of us being out, but we struggle if the pair of us are missing. We have similar roles in terms of linking the defence with the forwards, and Neil Webb is not as strong defensively. If Ince had stayed free of injuries he would have given us some crucial drive. He had hit top form at the time of his injury.

Two days later I went to see United at Luton. I am not particularly at ease watching the lads anyway, but once things started to go wrong it was agonising. Ince and myself were definitely missed in the game at Luton. United took the lead through Sharpe and had Ince or I been out there, I don't think we would have lost. In the event, we conceded a lame goal and lost Paul Parker, victim of a recurring hamstring injury, for the rest of the season. We went into the game with Forest with our confidence further stretched.

Our display against Forest was the best in the period dubbed 'Black Easter'. We created and missed a hatful of chances, but Forest took theirs with

Brian McClair's 100th goal of his United career was perfectly timed. *Below:* **Brian takes a fine pass from Giggs and holds off Williams to slide the ball home, as Walker, sent the wrong way by Giggs, looks on.**

clinical efficiency. That meant we had to win at Upton Park. The tension had increased and we gave a poor display. I felt wretched knowing I could not help the lads on the pitch, where it mattered. For them, the toll of playing on Thursday, Saturday, Monday and then Wednesday was too draining. The lads were exhausted before they even took the field.

A terrible disappointment

It is easier for the back players, because they spend periods of the game around the half-way line without having to get forward, but our midfield and forwards had to work up and down for 90 minutes *and* try to find some creative inspiration. That was why the goals dried up. In addition, I could not believe how much West Ham's fans wanted United to lose the title. Some of them were very aggressive to our players — and we lost to a goal that could have come from a slapstick comedy. The hardest part was accepting that we were no longer in the driving seat.

The build-up to the Anfield game was excruciatingly painful. I told Alex I was prepared to play — even if I broke down after 45 minutes. Ince felt the same way. I had not trained for a month, and my calf was not right, but I just could not bear to sit and watch another key game. We saw Leeds/Sheffield United, and seeing Sheffield give away such pathetic goals was hard to stomach. Leeds did well to win, though. It was hard going into the Liverpool game in a positive frame of mind — but we did. We felt Leeds

would win their last game, but we gave a good account of ourselves and only the woodwork — three times! — prevented a memorable win.

There was a terrible atmosphere in the dressing room after the game. I just yanked on my clothes and made straight for the coach. The atmosphere around the club in the week after was like a wake, but the Boss was great to us. He said that we had not let him down. He felt the disappointment as keenly as anyone, as he put it: 'Death is just about how I felt after seeing the title slip away. I undoubtedly feel that I have let the fans down, betrayed them almost.'

The lads did a tremendous job in the final match of the season, beating Spurs, but it showed the difference that having a free week made. We looked bright, played good passing football and pulled Tottenham apart. Sparky scored two goals in a 3-1 win. In the last six months of the season Mark had not been playing to his best, and had come in for a hell of a lot of criticism. But Mark would have been superhuman if he had been able to keep up the standard that had earned him the 'Player of the Year' award twice in three years. His endeavour is limitless, and he was credited with 14 'assists' during the season, but sometimes Alex will drop Sparky to get a reaction, and Hughes comes back fighting to do well.

Even though we faded, I still think we deserved to win the title. Howard Wilkinson said Leeds were the superior team, but in eight games since Leeds returned to the First Division, they have not beaten us. Although I think *we* were the better side, the League does not work like that, because we don't play Leeds 42 times. They deserve credit for the way

THE DOC'S DIAGNOSIS

Former Manchester United manager Tommy Docherty explained, in an interview for this book, why he thought the title eluded United: 'Alex Ferguson did a magnificent job winning three cups, and his pre-season signings — Parker, Schmeichel and Kanchelskis — were masterful buys. Peter Schmeichel, who I rate as the best 'keeper in the world, kept about 20 clean-sheets, but you have to put the ball in the back of the net. United didn't take their chances.

It would have been interesting to have seen Alex make a short-term buy. The great thing about being a successful manager is that you can buy players when things are going smoothly. McClair has done well scoring so many goals from deep, but Mark Hughes has not had a lot of support up front. Mark has never been a prolific goalscorer, so he needs a poacher up alongside him. Someone like John

Aldridge could have made a difference. Tranmere could have been persuaded to release him, and Aldo would probably have scored those crucial extra goals. United would have recouped the transfer fee with the added revenue from being in the European Cup.

The Old Trafford pitch was also a factor. It was not in a good condition, and a better home playing surface may have been worth around nine points. United are a good passing team and they found it tough to deal with the poor surface. It's hard to get skilful players to hump the ball up the field.

Alex was also caught in two minds about what his best team was, and some of the chopping and changing may have thrown the team off balance, but make no mistake about it — Leeds United didn't win the championship, Manchester United threw it away. The Reds had in it their grasp several times — Leeds only had that advantage

once, right at the end, and there weren't enough games left for any real pressure to build up on them.

There is no doubt that United missed Robson. He is a great captain and a magnificent player. I was sorry for him, because nobody in the game deserves the title medal more than him. But Robbo still has time get the medal he deserves. His biggest test will be keeping himself free of injuries. Handled probably he can be a major part of United's challenge. That might mean nursing him now and again if he gets a bit of a knock.

Winning the Premier League will be harder, however, because Leeds have strengthened their squad, and Arsenal and Liverpool will be more forceful. But if United's players show the right attitude and Alex Ferguson holds his nerve, they'll win it. The great pity of 1992 was that United blew their best chance for 25 years.'

they kept going all season, even when they had bad results, but Leeds did not win the title — we lost it.

Leeds had the League alone to concentrate on after we knocked them out of the two Cups, and in one winter week, when they had no Cup matches, they were able to go on a golfing holiday to Spain to recharge their batteries. It is no coincidence that four of our six defeats came during the time of our fixture pile-up. United were punished for being successful in other competitions. If we had made further progress in the FA Cup it would have been impossible to have fitted in every game before 2nd May. The Boss would probably have had to turn out for us.

For the first time since I've been a player, every club had to finish their League programme before 2nd May. If we had been able to go a week after the FA Cup Final, we would have steered ourselves home, because we would have had time to rest and get players fit and prepared for matches. When players are tired, physically and mentally, anxiety creeps in, and fear is a very corrosive emotion.

Opposite: **Mark Hughes withstands a challenge from Liverpool's Nicky Tanner in our defeat at Anfield, which sealed the title for Leeds.** *Below:* **A happier memory, as Ryan Giggs (*left*) and Gary Pallister, flanked by Alex Ferguson, collect their PFA awards.**

Despite the disappointment, there were reasons to feel pleased. Our defence was exceptional, conceding only 33 goals, the best record in Division One. Peter Schmeichel was a revelation. He later showed, in the brilliant way he helped Denmark win the European Championship in June 1992, his world-class ability. The Boss deserves a gold medal for that transfer, because Peter was one of the snatches of the decade.

Having a team that gives nothing away is a basis for future success, but we have to improve our scoring rate. Taking chances is what football is all about, and we let ourselves down on that front. But we also took heart from our supporters, who were fantastic, particularly in the last two months. They could not have done more to try and help us over the finishing line. It was the best support I have seen in 11 seasons as a Manchester United player.

Although we missed out on the title, and 25 years became 26, we are still the team setting the highest standards at the moment, because we have won three trophies in three years and no other side has done that. We have become a team in the fullest sense of the word and when United play to our potential then we can beat anyone. Our championship dream will remain just that unless we act decisively. Our task is to sustain that potential over a whole campaign, and then the League Championship will be ours.

MY UNITED DAYS

Becoming a Manchester United player is an enormous challenge for anyone, and I had the additional pressure of being Britain's most expensive player. I thought I could put all the headlines about my price tag to the back of my mind, but it was harder than I'd anticipated. At West Brom the spotlight had not been on me, but at United I found myself thinking: 'I shouldn't be making a bad pass like that, not for the money I cost!' I became over-anxious and tried to compensate, but that seemed to make it even worse, because I was just running round and round the pitch, as if I could justify the transfer by sweating blood.

In the end I said to myself: 'What is the point of trying too hard, and worrying so much, when you are playing poorly anyway?' So I forced myself to relax. I was also helped enormously by returning from the 1982 World Cup Finals full of confidence. I had scored the fastest goal in the history of the World Cup and had had a good tournament. I gave a particularly pleasing display against France, Michel Platini and all. From then on, my anxiety about the fee melted away. I'd learned some valuable lessons, and ever since have enjoyed my football, tried my best and played to win — that is all anyone can do.

I was bowled over by our fans

Being Britain's most expensive player is a big burden. Eight years after my transfer, Gary Pallister faced the same ordeal. In his first game for United, at home to Norwich, we played really badly and you could see it was making him over-anxious, and he gave away a penalty. He told the Press he was finding it hard to cope with the price tag, and having been through the same thing I knew I should help him. I had a friendly word with Gary, told him: 'You are a top-class player, don't worry about how much you cost. The Gaffer would not have paid that much unless he was convinced of your ability.' Once Gary grew in confidence, his skill saw him through — and our fans acknowledged that at the end of the season by voting him 'Player of the Year'. It's not a pressure that is exclusive to United — Liverpool's Dean Saunders also found it hard to handle. Most players are ordinary working class lads, and it can be difficult to mentally accept you are worth £3 million.

While I was bowled over by how friendly and enthusiastic fans were to me when I joined United, one thing I found hard to understand in my first season was the hate mail I received. Over the years I

Here, I evade Laurent Blanc's sliding tackle during the first leg of our Cup Winners' Cup quarter-final against Montpellier in 1991. Playing in Europe has been one of the most rewarding parts of my career.

111

have got used to it, and I have a secretary at the club now who puts abusive letters straight in the bin.

Ron Atkinson, who brought me to United, was very understanding and helpful to me in my early career, particularly when people harped on about my injury record. It has been a disappointment that injuries have prevented me from helping United at critical periods, but although I have missed over two years' worth of playing during my career, I have still notched up a high number of matches — I am in the top ten of Manchester United's postwar appearances.

Helping new team-mates

The reason my injuries have attracted so much over-the-top publicity is because I missed some big games for United, including two League Cup Finals, and had to return early from two World Cup Finals as England's captain. I have been unlucky with injuries as far as missing some really important matches goes, but I'm sure that many players would liked to have gone up the Wembley steps three times to collect the FA Cup. It also gives me great satisfaction that as I approach my late 30s, I am still playing at the highest level — in the 1992-93 season I will pass the 800 mark of games at first-class and international level.

There must have been a few forests lost providing the paper for all those silly diagrams of my body with arrows pointing to injuries, but the only time I have ever been really angered by an article about my fitness record was when I read one by Emlyn Hughes. He reckoned that I don't know how to tackle, and that's why I suffer so many injuries. It is the biggest load of rubbish I have ever read about myself. In the 1976-77 season, when I was coming up to 20, I broke my leg three times. The first was because of a mistimed tackle, but the next fracture was the result of playing after coming back too quickly. But at United, nearly all my injuries have occurred when there has been no one near me. A few have been the result of over-stretching; and the dislocation happened when I fell over advertising hoardings during a game at Old Trafford. I tore my ankle ligaments in the 1983 League Cup semi-final second leg against Arsenal (the injury that kept me out of the League Cup Final against Liverpool), by twisting my ankle as I jumped for the ball on a frozen pitch at Old Trafford. Nearly all these have been the result of physical movement and strain, and not any flaw in my method of tackling, so I knew that Emlyn Hughes had not even bothered to find out the full story. Another absurd article claimed that I didn't know how to fall, but I certainly knew how to fall when I crashed over those hoardings!

Recovering from an injury provides plenty of time for reflection — that can be productive if you use it positively, but many players find it a hard, lonely time, when they brood a lot. I was brought up never

Beating Barcelona 3-0 at Old Trafford in March 1984, in which I scored twice, was one of the most pleasurable games of my life. *Right:* **Jose Moratalla gets out of the way of one of my shots that night.**

to feel sorry for myself and it's an attitude I have applied during those periods of recovery. I have been under the knife a fair few times in my life, but fortunately I'm not squeamish — where there is no sense there is no feeling, I suppose!

Whether players are in the team or at home recuperating, it is their families that help them cope with the strain of a footballer's life. My family are the heart of my life, which made receiving the OBE in the Queen's 1990 New Year's Honours list a special award. I have won numerous medals in football, but the OBE was one that my family could all share in.

Denise, my wife, hardly ever talks about football to me — not because she is uninterested, but because she and I agree on the benefit of not bringing work into the home. It is not always possible for me to detach myself from football, and the adrenaline is still flowing long after some games. This is why I like going out for a meal and having a couple of drinks after a game. If you have a few drinks then, when you are drained anyway, it takes effect quickly. That helps me switch off and get to sleep. You have to find ways to relax — it's counterproductive to be hyped up about football all the time. When that happens a person becomes a bit stereotyped and loses some of his enthusiasm. I know a lot of players feel this way.

During my United career I have seen dozens of players come and go, and in my role as captain I have

CAPTAIN MARVEL

Ron Atkinson said, in an interview for Glory Glory Man United!: 'Bryan is the complete midfield player. He deserves his nickname of 'Captain Marvel', because of his bravery and spirit, but he also has great skill and a deep understanding of the game, which will serve him well in the future. I put him up there along with the all-time greats like Dave McKay and Duncan Edwards. Some people questioned the wisdom of breaking the British transfer record to buy him, yet within two years his value had doubled.

Now, some 11 years after I signed him, Robbo is still a vital part of United's team. The injury to Bryan was one of the deciding factors in why Manchester United failed to win the title in 1992. Aston Villa played them twice at opposite ends of the season and we lost twice. The reason we lost both games was because United had Robson. He was the difference between the two teams. His influence was apparent in the results United had when they were without him. While he was in the team they hardly lost a League game, yet they faltered when he was out injured. He is the kind of player who makes a good team great.

Bryan drives a team. A lot of players look to him for inspiration. His personal courage is staggering and he is a born leader. I have seen him tear a strip off superstar team-mates if they weren't doing their stuff and I have seen him orchestrate the flow of play on the field with the subtlest of hand signals. There is nobody you would rather have out there as captain.

The factor that is most striking about Bryan is his competitive nature. That is why he is still pushing himself and the team at his age, and although he is special on the field, he is down-to-earth and pleasant off it — but it will be burning him up to win that League Championship medal. If anyone can help United win it is Captain Marvel.'

tried to do my best to help them, on and off the pitch. I like to make new players feel welcome at United. For quite a few years I have hosted a barbecue every summer for all the players and their partners. Bert Millichip, my Chairman at West Brom, used to organise a similar event, and they were always enjoyable. Many signings are made in the summer and it is thus a good way for a new team-mate and his family to get to know everyone in the squad. People have a few drinks, loosen up and chat more easily. This is important for a player's partner as well, because when new players arrive at Old Trafford, there is a strong chance that they won't know anyone in the northwest (something Denise and I encountered when we built a new life together in Manchester). It is often a player's wife who bears the brunt of the changes, especially if babies and young children are on the scene, because she might have moved away from her friends, family and trusted babysitter! Moreover, she isn't escaping every morning to go training with the lads. But most senior pros will make a big effort to help new players — after all, we have all been in the same boat.

My major role as captain is on the field. I want to win every game I take part in and I expect the same commitment from my team-mates. If I occasionally have to shout at a few to remind them of this, then I will bark at them. Usually I can rely on just having quiet words with colleagues, and it is always refreshing to see that people do actually respond to simple words of encouragement. I have matured with age, too, and have developed greater patience with younger players than I had even five years ago. I appreciate that they need a bit of help and that shouting at them all the time may actually discourage them from doing the right things.

Great managers get the best out of a side, because they make players want to play for them. No player is a machine who can simply be switched on and expected to turn out the goods automatically — and the manager has to get the spirit right in a team. Footballers are as mixed as people in any other walk of life, and as varied in their intelligence and character as they are in their talent. Friction can make a dressing room a horrible place, but at United, the teams I have played in have had superb spirit. When everyone is pulling together, there is a great sense of dedication and comradeship. What can spoil that is one bad apple but, happily, the two United bosses I have played under have been sharp judges of character, able to spot a troublemaker.

Alex Ferguson is probably a bit harder than Ron — but he is scrupulously dedicated to the whole team. He thinks of Manchester United, not sensibilities, and reputations count for nothing with him. Alex is a very thorough man and his preparation for games is first rate. He watches the opposition carefully, and pays particular attention to their set pieces. Neil Webb told me that Brian Clough, his former Boss, would just stroll in before the kickoff and say: 'Enjoy the match — have a good game.' Alex would never be that laid-back. He is a workaholic, always into the club first thing, planning and preparing. Both Ron and Alex also know how to pick good deputies, and Mick Brown, who came with Ron, and Archie Knox, were excellent at organising training.

Alex is very different in temperament to Big Ron. Atkinson rarely displayed what he felt, whether in triumph or despair. Alex is much more inclined to show publicly what he is feeling, and display his emotional ups and downs. What they have in common is that both live, eat and sleep the game — and I have had some of my most enjoyable conversations about football with them.

Both have been very supportive in my career as a player, although Ron certainly had more influence because he knew me when I was still developing. I never looked at one player and thought: 'I want to copy his style', but I really admired Bobby Moore, Bobby Moncur, Norman Hunter, Colin Todd and Kevin Beattie — I used to like the way they played and their ability to read the game. But I never fancied being an attacker, even though George Best is my all-time favourite player.

Memorable games for the Reds

Making long runs was a natural part of my game, but when I was a lad there were numerous skills and techniques that I practised very hard — especially those to strengthen playing with my right foot. I was fairly small when I was in my early teens, and people were worried about me getting injured, so I did extra weight training, sprinting and cross country to build myself up. That was from about 15-18 and it really paid off. Kids of that age should work very hard at developing stamina and building their hearts and lungs while they are still growing.

Gordon Strachan, Kevin Moran, Ray Wilkins and Cyrille Regis, former team-mates of mine, were all great trainers and worked hard when they were teenagers and as a result, although they are in their mid-30s, they are still playing at the top level. A lot of players have retired prematurely because, after a few bad displays, they listened to their critics and let themselves go in training. We have all been helped by knowing more about diet and as long as you enjoy the game and enjoy training, your mind will help your body over the fitness hurdles. As I have got older, a lot of people have said I should play as a

sweeper, a role I had at 18 for the England Youth team when we won the mini World Cup. I considered playing in central defence when I first started out, and played in lots of different roles for West Brom.

Alex Ferguson has been happy to let me play in the same way that I had under Atkinson. The Boss has occasionally used me in defence, and although I prefer being in midfield, I am quite capable of playing as a sweeper or alongside the centre-half, or in front of the back four, rather than behind them. I have played as a sweeper in certain away games for Alex, when it suits his strategy for a particular game; we've had good results using that system.

Experience helps, because being a sweeper is largely a matter of reading the game. Intercepting opponents is a hard skill to master, but when you perform it well it is as satisfying as making a strong run upfield or getting in a good shot. Glenn Hoddle has played in that role for Swindon, which disproves the theory that you have to have someone who is a brilliant tackler in the role. United can only really use the sweeper in away games, forcing teams to come out and attack. It would not work at Old Trafford, where we often come up against teams who leave nine men behind the ball. They would let you pass the ball around your defence all day, and a sweeper would simply be a wasted player.

Looking back over more than 400 games for Manchester United fills me with deep delight and few things have given me more pleasure in life than lifting the European Cup Winners' Cup. Out of all those matches, that 1991 victory against Barcelona would certainly be in my favourite five, and would rate as one of my finest performances for United.

Barcelona were also the opposition for another of those five — when we came back from a first leg two-goal deficit in 1984 to win 3-0 in the quarter-final of the same competition. There is always something brilliant about European nights, but that was special, because of the atmosphere created by our fans — the best I've experienced at Old Trafford — and Bobby Charlton and Matt Busby were there to enjoy it.

Top: **United's fans carry me off after our momentous win against Barcelona in 1984.** *Opposite:* **I'll always cherish my long-range goal in the 1985 FA Cup semi-final replay against Liverpool. I broke through their offside trap — and it is critical in that situation that you hold your nerve. I knew that Ronnie Whelan was close behind me, so I had to beat him or shoot from afar. Happily, I curled a screamer into the net.**

Another of the quintet would be the 1983 FA Cup Final replay against Brighton, because of the sheer confidence and assurity with which we played with that night. I scored two goals, and our fourth goal — a penalty — was the result of a foul on me. Only Stan Mortensen, for Blackpool in 1953, has scored a hat-trick in an FA Cup Final this century, and it did cross my mind that I would achieve a rare feat if I scored from the kick — and as captain, the decision was mine. But Arnold Muhren was United's penalty taker that season, and if we had been 1-0 down and been awarded a spot kick he would have taken it. It would have been really harsh, not to say egotistical, of me to take away his chance of scoring at Wembley in an FA Cup Final. In addition, I don't think Arnold would ever have spoken to me again if I had taken the penalty and missed!

Another great performance was the 1985 FA Cup semi-final replay. In the first leg at Goodison, we were 2-1 up, from goals by Stapleton and myself, and had been within a minute of winning, but Liverpool had equalised. We could have been really deflated, thinking fate was against us, but we produced a really sterling performance in the replay, after going behind, and Sparky and I netted excellent goals.

The League game I enjoyed most came in March 1992, when we beat Sheffield United at Bramall Lane. I was happy with the way we played and enjoyed my role — going back to our defence, collecting the ball and setting up fluent passing movements. We did that throughout the game and even though we went a goal down I felt sure we would win; it is unusual to get a strong feeling like that when you are one behind. Alan Cork said that United were 'boring', but that was no surprise as he'd spent the game running in between our defenders to try and get the

ball, and it is murder if you are a striker and you have to spend 90 minutes chasing the ball. We played some masterful possession football that day.

Not all of my games have been memorable. I think my worst game for United was against Newcastle United at St James's Park, and it was under Alex Ferguson. I did not do a thing right. I gave the ball away all the time and never got near winning a tackle. It was a shocking display. I should have donated my wages to charity that week.

It has been interesting playing with so many superb players and different teams. The side Ron created in 1983 was one of the best attacking teams I have been part of, but the team of 1991-1992 takes some beating. That side produced the best winning streak in the modern history of the club — capturing a trophy for three consecutive years. The current United side is the hardest to beat of all the ones I have played with, and has rid itself of a lot of the inconsistency that used to hold us back.

The third FA Cup win was best

Fans used to ask me whether winning the FA Cup was better the first or second time, but it did not feel any different. The third triumph *did* feel better, not because it meant I had created a new record — as the only captain to lift the FA Cup three times at Wembley — but because I was so delighted for the new players and the young lads in the squad. In 1983 and 1985, my team-mates had been around the same age and had won medals before, but for many of the 1990 side it was their first honour and particularly gratifying after all the stick we had taken that season.

United do attract a lot of criticism, and you have to learn to shrug it off. That is really hard for the manager of Manchester United, especially when the Press start implying that he ought to be sacked. That is not 'reporting'. The manager's position is a matter for the Board of Directors. What really gets on my nerves is when ex-professionals take money for criticising players in the tabloids. The articles are not written for the benefit of the players, and it upsets me, because the people who indulge in that have been pros themselves, earned a good living from football and should have more respect for the game.

To the Press it's just ammunition in their constant circulation war. Headlines about players moving also attract readers — and I have been the subject of numerous stories of this ilk during my career. You could fill a new Premier League with a list of clubs I have been 'set to join' in the last 11 years.

The only move that had any real substance was when I might have ended up in Italy in 1984. All the rest have been absolute eyewash! I have never been in touch with other clubs about leaving United. When Gary Lineker signed up to go to Grampas Eight in Japan, there was some interest from Japan, but I simply wasn't interested in going to the Far East. I had no desire to leave United and intend to continue playing First Division football for as long as possible. Furthermore, I hope to make my next career as a manager, so it would not be right for me to go away

115

MY UNITED GREATS

During my career with Manchester United I've had the rare privilege of teaming up with some of the best players in the modern game. In all, I played with 73 team-mates in my first 11 seasons at Old Trafford — all of them special in their own way. As you can imagine, the task of choosing my top side and whittling down a long list of great talents was agonising work, but I helped myself by choosing five subs — and gave myself a bit of room there, too, because I left a spare 'keeper off the bench. I would like to express my thanks to all my current and former United team-mates and apologise to those not in the final 'Team of Greats', but there was certainly no lack of choice. I must have gone through a box of pencils drawing up the selection, and I could have picked about five world-class teams. In some cases the process of elimination was easier — Peter Schmeichel, for example, even after only one season, stands out as the best of the 10 'keepers I have played with at United — but choosing a midfield from a list that included Coppell, Ince, Macari, McIlroy, Moses, Muhren, Olsen, Phelan, Strachan and Webb, was really tough (my editor insisted that I went in the side!). This was the final team I decided on:

1: Peter Schmeichel; 2: Paul Parker; 3: Denis Irwin; 4: Ray Wilkins; 5: Gary Pallister; 6: Paul McGrath; 7: Bryan Robson; 8: Steve Coppell; 9: Mark Hughes; 10: Norman Whiteside; 11: Ryan Giggs. Subs: Steve Bruce, Arnold Muhren, Gordon Strachan, Paul Ince and Brian McClair.

I like challenges. I want success as a player — and I want it when I become a manager. I realise that the pressure on managers is greater than on players, but I am happy to take on that burden. I have taken a lot of criticism in my career, and that has hardened me. You can either retire from the game or you can accept the challenge — drawbacks and all. The prospect of criticism won't put me off.

Although there has been a great deal of speculation that I would take up a position as a player-manager somewhere, I wanted to continue playing and concentrate solely on that. As a young player you can sometimes sail through training and keep fit easily, while in your middle 30s you need extreme discipline to maintain a level of fitness to be able to compete in the most physical and fast League in the world.

Football is as important to me now as it was when I started out. Perhaps I am still especially fired up because of not having won the championship. Every team sets off to win the League. We took a lot of stick a few seasons ago, but ended up winning three trophies. We have some fine young players and I am relishing seeing all of them coming through to prove themselves. That will make it easier to win the title.

Missing out on the title in 1992 was the biggest disappointment of my United career, but nobody gets through a career in football without a few broken dreams. I had felt that it was definitely going to be our season, but the important thing for us is to learn from the experience, so we will be stronger than before. Looking back at the season, game by game, result by result, I feel that what we were doing was fundamentally on the right lines but we were punished by the fixture pile-up and injuries, and hindered ourselves by not scoring. At any level of football it comes down to taking chances and we didn't do that — with even slight progress, success will come. I was happy with my form that season and just disappointed with my calf injury. I played as well in 1991-92 as I ever have and still enjoy training. Although I am older, I look after myself better — and don't have a sore head so often in the mornings!

I don't feel envy towards any player who has won a championship medal, because every player who has won one has worked hard for it. Sometimes you can't win everything in life. I have been fortunate as a player in the medals and recognition that I have won. It is still my chief ambition to win a League title medal as a player — but if I don't, then I will certainly be trying my best to win one as a manager. You can only give your best. That may not be good enough at the end of the day, but as long as you can hold your head up and say 'I tried my best', then the fans will recognise your effort.

I will get to the end of the 1992-93 season and see how training has gone, and how my form has been. If I am playing well enough and feel fit enough, then I will consider playing on. I would probably look to go by annual contracts, because I don't want to play on if I feel my fitness waning. If I can't do the job at the highest level for United there is no point in me being at the club. But one thing is for sure: there will be no one trying harder than me to end my 16th First Division season by helping United's marvellous fans to celebrate a League Championship triumph.

from the English scene at the moment, because I need to be up-to-date with all the players.

At the end of the 1990-91 season there was a lot of speculation about my position, but there was never a doubt about me leaving United. The Boss said he had no intention of letting me go, and I was happy to sign a new two-year contract. When I read this sort of gossip, I let it run off my back. It has been going on for so many years now. As a footballer to preserve any sanity you might have started with you have to limit the number of people whose opinion can affect you. Unless they care for you, or have done you some good, then their views don't matter.

A few years ago I decided that when I do pack up playing I will try and go into management. I have always voiced my opinions to managers — although whether they have listened or not is another matter! I am the sort of person who has strong views on the game, and players like me think our judgment is as good as anyone else's — but the only way you can actually prove that is to go into management yourself and make a success of it. All the experience I have gathered as a player will come in useful, and I have learned as many valuable lessons from bad seasons as from good ones — and I could not have had a better place to learn than at Manchester United.

United's fans have always been great to me, and over 40,000 fans turned up for my testimonial against Celtic at Old Trafford in November 1990. *Opposite:* I'm with my daughters Clare (right) and Charlotte.

MAN UNITED STATISTICS: 1981-92

HONOURS RECORD

Football League Division One: *Champions* 1907-08, 1910-11, 1951-52, 1955-56, 1956-57, 1964-65, 1966-67; *Runners-up* 1946-47, 1947-48, 1948-49, 1950-51, 1958-59, 1963-64, 1967-68, 1979-80, 1987-88, 1991-92

Football League Division Two: *Champions* 1935-36, 1974-75; *Runners-up* 1896-97, 1905-06, 1924-25, 1937-38

FA Cup: *Winners* 1909, 1948, 1963, 1977, 1983, 1985, 1990; *Finalists* 1957, 1958, 1976, 1979

Football League Cup (now Rumbelows League Cup): *Winners* 1992; *Finalists* 1983, 1991

European Cup: *Winners* 1968

European Cup Winners' Cup: *Winners* 1991

European Super Cup: *Winners* 1991

FA Charity Shield: *Winners* 1908, 1911, 1952, 1956, 1957, 1983; *Joint Holders* 1965, 1967, 1977, 1990; *Finalists* 1948, 1963, 1985

FA Youth Cup: *Winners* 1953, 1954, 1955, 1956, 1957, 1964, 1992; *Finalists* 1982, 1986

RON ATKINSON'S TRANSFER RECORD (July 1981 to November 1986)

BOUGHT			SOLD		
1: John Gidman	from Everton	for £450,000	1: Joe Jordan	to A.C. Milan	for £170,000
2: Frank Stapleton	from Arsenal	for £900,000	2: Mickey Thomas	to Everton	for £450,000
3: Remi Moses	from WBA	for £500,000	3: Sammy McIlroy	to Stoke City	for £350,000
4: Bryan Robson	from WBA	for £1.8 m	4: Jimmy Nicholl	to Toronto	for £253,000
5: Paul McGrath	from St Patrick's	for £25,000	5: Tom Connell	to Glentoran	for £37,500
6: Arnold Muhren	from Ipswich Town	free transfer	6: Paddy Roche	to Brentford	for £15,000
7: Peter Bodak	from Coventry City	free transfer	7: Garry Birtles	to Nott'm Forest	for £275,000
8: Peter Beardsley	from Van. Whitecaps	for £250,000	8: Peter Beardsley	to Van. Whitecaps	for £250,000
9: Arthur Graham	from Leeds United	for £65,000	9: Peter Bodak	to Manchester City	free transfer
10: Alan Brazil	from Tottenham	for £700,000	10: Ashley Grimes	to Coventry City	for £200,000
11: Jesper Olsen	from Ajax	for £800,000	11: Martin Buchan	to Oldham Athletic	free transfer
12: Gordon Strachan	from Aberdeen	for £600,000	12: Scott McGarvey	to Portsmouth	for £85,000
13: Chris Turner	from Sunderland	for £275,000	13: Ray Wilkins	to A.C. Milan	for £1.5 m
14: Colin Gibson	from Aston Villa	for £312,000	14: David Platt	to Crewe Alexandra	for £50,000
15: Peter Barnes	from Coventry City	for £55,000	15: Arthur Graham	to Bradford City	for £10,000
16: Terry Gibson	from Coventry City	for £630,000	16: Stephen Pears	to Middlesbrough	for £85,000
17: Peter Davenport	from Nott'm Forest	for £600,000	17: Alan Davies	to Newcastle United	for £65,000
18: John Sivebaek	from Vejle	for £285,000	18: Alan Brazil	to Coventry City	for £280,000
19: Joe Hanrahan	from U.C. Dublin	for £30,000	19: Mark Hughes	to Barcelona	for £1.8 m
20: Mark Higgins	from Everton	for £58,500	20: Mark Dempsey	to Sheffield United	for £4,500
21: Liam O'Brien	from Bohemians	for £72,500	21: John Gidman	to Manchester City	free transfer

Total spent = £8,408,000	**Total received = £5,880,000**

There have been many great moments for me at United, including the time I lifted the FA Cup after our 1-0 win against Everton in 1985 *(right)*.

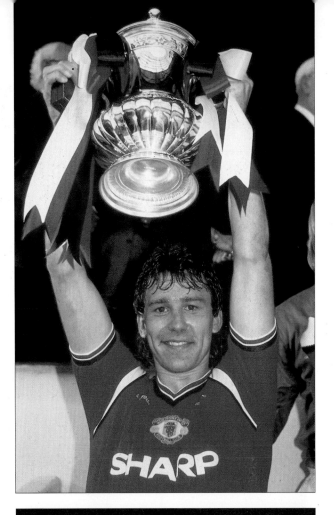

ROBSON'S CAREER RECORD

West Bromwich Albion (1974/75 to 1981/82)

League appearances (including as a sub):	197
League goals:	39
FA Cup appearances (including as a sub):	12
FA Cup goals:	2
League Cup appearances (including as a sub):	18
League Cup goals:	2
European competition appearances:	12
European competition goals:	2
Total appearances (including as a sub)	243
Total goals:	45

Manchester United (1981/82 to 1991/92)

League appearances (including as a sub):	316
League goals:	72
FA Cup appearances:	32
FA Cup goals:	8
League Cup appearances (including as a sub):	45
League Cup goals:	5
European competition appearances:	18
European competition goals:	7
Total appearances (including as a sub)	411
Total goals:	93

England international career (1980-1991)
Debut: Against the Republic of Ireland at Wembley on 6th February 1980.
Total caps: 90 (including 63 as captain).
Total goals: 27.
Appearances: *1980* — Republic of Ireland, Australia, *1981*— Norway, Romania, Switzerland, Spain, Romania, Brazil, Wales, Scotland, Switzerland, Hungary; *1982* — Norway (1), Hungary, Northern Ireland (1). **[With United]** Wales, Holland, Spain, Scotland, Finland (2), France (2), Czechoslovakia, West Germany; *1983* — Denmark, Greece, Luxembourg, Scotland (1); *1984* — Hungary, Luxembourg (2), France, Northern Ireland, Scotland, USSR, Brazil, Uruguay, Chile; *1985* — East Germany (1), Finland (1), Turkey (3), Rep. Ireland, Mexico, West Germany (1), Romania, Finland, Scotland, Italy, United States; *1986* — Romania, Turkey (1), Israel (2), Mexico, Portugal, Morocco; *1987* — Northern Ireland, Spain, Northern Ireland (1), Turkey, Brazil, Scotland; *1988* — Turkey (1), Yugoslavia (1), Holland, Hungary, Scotland, Colombia, Switzerland, Rep. Ireland, Holland (1), USSR; *1989* — Sweden, Denmark, Saudi Arabia, Greece (1), Albania (1), Albania (1), Chile, Scotland, Poland, Denmark; *1990* — Poland, Italy, Yugoslavia (2), Czechoslovakia, Uruguay, Tunisia, Rep. Ireland, Holland; *1991* — Cameroon, Rep. Ireland, Turkey. (Goals in brackets).
England B: Three caps: 1979 — Austria; 1980 — Spain; 1990 — Algeria.
England Youth: One cap — 1975.
England Under-21: Seven caps, two goals: 1979 — Wales, Bulgaria, Sweden (1), Denmark, Bulgaria; 1980 — Scotland (1), Scotland.

MANCHESTER UNITED'S COMPLETE RECORD SEASON BY SEASON, FROM 1981/82 TO 1991/92, INCLUSIVE, INCLUDING DETAILS OF ALL FIRST-TEAM MATCHES

CODE

D1 — League Division One match; FA — FA Cup; LC — League Cup (later Milk Cup, Littlewoods Cup and Rumbelows League Cup); CS — Charity Shield; ECWC — European Cup Winners' Cup; ESC — European Super Cup; SF — Semi-final; F — Final; A — Away match; H — Home match; N — Neutral ground; W — Wembley; R — Replay

1981-82

Manager: Ron Atkinson
Played 45, **Won** 22, **Lost** 11, **Drawn** 12, **Goals for** 59, **Goals against** 32
Appearances (including as a substitute): Albiston, Wilkins 45; Stapleton 44; Bailey 42; Gidman 40; Coppell 38; Birtles 36; Robson 35; Moran 33; Buchan 30; Duxbury 25; Moses 23; McQueen 21; McGarvey 16; McIlroy 14; Macari 12; Grimes 11; Roche 3; Whiteside 2; Davies, Nicholl 1
Goals: Stapleton 13 (inc. 1 pen); Birtles 11; Coppell 9 (inc. 1 pen); Moran 7; Robson 5; McIlroy 3; Macari, McGarvey, Moses 2; Albiston, Gidman, Grimes, Whiteside, Wilkins 1

August

29 D1 Coventry City   A 1-2 Macari
31 D1 Nottingham Forest   H 0-0

September

5 D1 Ipswich Town   H 1-2 Stapleton
12 D1 Aston Villa   A 1-1 Stapleton
19 D1 Swansea City   H 1-0 Birtles
22 D1 Middlesbrough   A 2-0 Stapleton, Birtles
26 D1 Arsenal   A 0-0
30 D1 Leeds United   H 1-0 Stapleton

October

3 D1 Wolves   H 5-0 Stapleton, Birtles, McIlroy 3

7 LC Tottenham Hotspur   A 0-1
10 D1 Manchester City   A 0-0
17 D1 Birmingham City   H 1-1 Coppell
21 D1 Middlesbrough   H 1-0 Moses
24 D1 Liverpool   A 2-1 Moran, Albiston
28 LC Tottenham Hotspur   H 0-1
31 D1 Notts County   H 2-1 Birtles, Moses

November

7 D1 Sunderland   A 5-1 Moran, Robson, Stapleton 2, Birtles

21 D1 Tottenham Hotspur   A 1-3 Birtles
28 D1 Brighton   H 2-1 Birtles, Stapleton

December

5 D1 Southampton   A 2-3 Stapleton, Robson

January

2 FA Watford   A 0-1
6 D1 Everton   H 1-1 Stapleton
23 D1 Stoke City   A 3-0 Stapleton (pen), Birtles, Coppell,
27 D1 West Ham United   H 1-0 Macari
30 D1 Swansea City   A 0-2

February

6 D1 Aston Villa   H 4-1 Moran 2, Robson, Coppell

13 D1 Wolves   A 1-0 Birtles
20 D1 Arsenal   H 0-0
27 D1 Manchester City   H 1-1 Moran

March

6 D1 Birmingham City   A 1-0 Birtles
17 D1 Coventry City   H 0-1
20 D1 Notts County   A 3-1 Coppell 2, Stapleton

27 D1 Sunderland   H 0-0

April

3 D1 Leeds United   A 0-0
7 D1 Liverpool   H 0-1
10 D1 Everton   A 3-3 Coppell 2, Grimes
12 D1 West Bromwich Albion   H 1-0 Moran
17 D1 Tottenham Hotspur   H 2-0 Coppell (pen), McGarvey

20 D1 Ipswich Town   A 1-2 Gidman
24 D1 Brighton   A 1-0 Wilkins

May

1 D1 Southampton   H 1-0 McGarvey
5 D1 Nottingham Forest   A 1-0 Stapleton
8 D1 West Ham United   A 1-1 Moran
12 D1 West Bromwich Albion   A 3-0 Robson, Birtles, Coppell

15 D1 Stoke City   H 2-0 Robson, Whiteside

Final League position: 3rd

━━━ 1982-83 ━━━

Manager: Ron Atkinson
Played 60, **Won** 31, **Lost** 12, **Drawn** 17, **Goals for** 92, **Goals against** 51
Appearances (including as a substitute): Duxbury 60; Stapleton 59; Whiteside 57; Albiston 56; Bailey 55; McQueen 53; Robson 49; Muhren 46; Moran 44; Coppell, Moses 43; Wilkins 36; Grimes 21; McGrath 16; Macari 14; McGarvey 8; Buchan 6; Cunningham, Davies, Wealands 5; Gidman 3; Beardsley 1
Goals: Stapleton 19; Robson 15; Whiteside 14; Coppell 11 (inc. 2 pens); Muhren 7 (inc. 1 pen); Moran 5; McGrath, McQueen 3; Albiston, Grimes (inc. 1 pen), Macari, Moses, own goals, Wilkins 2; Cunningham, Duxbury, McGarvey 1

August

28 D1 Birmingham City   H 3-0 Moran, Stapleton, Coppell

September

1 D1 Nottingham Forest   A 3-0 Wilkins, Whiteside, Robson
4 D1 West Bromwich Albion   A 1-3 Robson
8 D1 Everton   H 2-1 Whiteside, Robson
11 D1 Ipswich Town   H 3-1 Whiteside 2, Coppell
15 UC Valencia   H 0-0
18 D1 Southampton   A 1-0 Macari
25 D1 Arsenal   H 0-0
29 UC Valencia   A 1-2 Robson

October

2 D1 Luton Town   A 1-1 Grimes
6 LC Bournemouth   H 2-0 Redknapp (o.g.), Stapleton

9 D1 Stoke City   H 1-0 Robson
16 D1 Liverpool   A 0-0
23 D1 Manchester City   H 2-2 Stapleton 2
26 LC Bournemouth   A 2-2 Muhren, Coppell (pen)
30 D1 West Ham United   A 1-3 Moran

November

6 D1 Brighton   A 0-1
10 LC Bradford City   A 0-0
13 D1 Tottenham Hotspur   H 1-0 Muhren
20 D1 Aston Villa   A 1-2 Stapleton
24 LC Bradford City   H 4-1 Moses, Albiston, Moran, Coppell

27 D1 Norwich City   H 3-0 Muhren, Robson 2

December

1 LC Southampton   H 2-0 McQueen, Whiteside
4 D1 Watford   A 1-0 Whiteside
11 D1 Notts County   H 4-0 Whiteside, Robson, Stapleton, Duxbury

18 D1 Swansea City   A 0-0
27 D1 Sunderland   H 0-0
28 D1 Coventry City   A 0-3

January

1 D1 Aston Villa   H 3-1 Stapleton 2, Coppell
3 D1 West Bromwich Albion   H 0-0
8 FA West Ham United   H 2-0 Stapleton, Coppell
15 D1 Birmingham City   A 2-1 Whiteside, Robson
19 LC Nottingham Forest   H 4-0 McQueen 2, Coppell, Robson

22 D1 Nottingham Forest   H 2-0 Coppell (pen), Muhren
29 FA Luton Town   A 2-0 Moses, Moran

February

5 D1 Ipswich Town   A 1-1 Stapleton
15 LCSF Arsenal   A 4-2 Whiteside, Stapleton, Coppell 2

19 FA Derby County	A 1-0	Whiteside
22 LCSF Arsenal	H 2-1	Coppell, Moran
26 D1 Liverpool	H 1-1	Muhren

March

2 D1 Stoke City	A 0-1	
5 D1 Manchester City	A 2-1	Stapleton 2
12 FA Everton	H 1-0	Stapleton
19 D1 Brighton	H 1-1	Albiston
22 D1 West Ham United	H 2-1	Stapleton, McGarvey
26 LCF Liverpool	W 1-2	Whiteside

April

2 D1 Coventry City	H 3-0	Stapleton, Gillespie (o.g.), Macari ·
4 D1 Sunderland	A 0-0	
9 D1 Southampton	H 1-1	Robson
16 FASF Arsenal	N 2-1	Robson, Whiteside
19 D1 Everton	A 0-2	
23 D1 Watford	H 2-0	Cunningham, Grimes (pen)
30 D1 Norwich City	A 1-1	Whiteside

May

2 D1 Arsenal	A 0-3	
7 D1 Swansea City	H 2-1	Robson, Stapleton
9 D1 Luton Town	H 3-0	McGrath 2, Stapleton
11 D1 Tottenham Hotspur	A 0-2	
14 D1 Notts County	A 2-3	McGrath, Moran
21 FAF Brighton	W 2-2	Stapleton, Wilkins
26 FAFR Brighton	W 4-0	Robson 2, Whiteside, Muhren

Final League position: 3rd **Won FA Cup**
Finalists Milk Cup

━━━━━━ **1983-84** ━━━━━━

Manager: Ron Atkinson
Played 58, **Won** 27, **Lost** 12, **Drawn** 19, **Goals for** 93, **Goals against** 56
Appearances (including as a substitute): Stapleton 58; Albiston, Wilkins 56; Bailey, Duxbury 55; Moran 52; Graham, Whiteside 51; Moses, Robson 47; Muhren 35; McQueen 29; Hughes 17; McGrath 13; Gidman, Macari 10; Crooks 7; Hogg 6; Davies 4; Wealands 3; Blackmore 1
Goals: Stapleton 19, Robson 18; Whiteside 12; Muhren 8 (inc. 4 pens); Graham, Moran 7; Hughes, Wilkins 5 (inc. 2 pens); Moses 3; Albiston, Crooks, McQueen 2; Davies, Hogg, McGrath 1

August

20 CS Liverpool	W 2-0	Robson 2
27 D1 Queen's Park Rangers	H 3-1	Muhren 2 (inc. 1 pen), Stapleton
29 D1 Nottingham Forest	H 1-2	Moran

September

3 D1 Stoke City	A 1-0	Muhren
6 D1 Arsenal	A 3-2	Moran, Robson, Stapleton
10 D1 Luton Town	H 2-0	Muhren (pen), Albiston
14 ECWC Dulka Prague	H 1-1	Wilkins
17 D1 Southampton	A 0-3	
24 D1 Liverpool	H 1-0	Stapleton
27 ECWC Dulka Prague	A 2-2	Stapleton, Robson

October

1 D1 Norwich City	A 3-3	Whiteside 2, Stapleton
3 LC Port Vale	A 1-0	Stapleton
15 D1 West Bromwich Albion	H 3-0	Albiston, Graham, Whiteside
19 ECWC JSK Spartak Varna	A 2-1	Robson, Graham

22 D1 Sunderland	A 1-0	Wilkins (pen)
26 LC Port Vale	H 2-0	Wilkins (pen), Whiteside
29 D1 Wolves	H 3-0	Stapleton 2, Robson

November

2 ECWC JSK Spartak Varna	H 2-0	Stapleton 2
5 D1 Aston Villa	H 1-2	Robson
8 LC Colchester United	A 2-0	McQueen, Moses
12 D1 Leicester City	A 1-1	Robson
19 D1 Watford	H 4-1	Stapleton 3, Robson
27 D1 West Ham United	A 1-1	Wilkins
30 LC Oxford United	A 1-1	Hughes

December

3 D1 Everton	H 0-1	
7 LC Oxford United	H 1-1	Stapleton
10 D1 Ipswich Town	A 2-0	Graham, Crooks
16 D1 Tottenham Hotspur	H 4-2	Moran 2, Graham 2
19 LC Oxford United	A 1-2	Graham
26 D1 Coventry City	A 1-1	Muhren (pen)
27 D1 Notts County	H 3-3	Crooks, McQueen, Moran
31 D1 Stoke City	H 1-0	Graham

January

2 D1 Liverpool	A 1-1	Whiteside
7 FA Bournemouth	A 0-2	
13 D1 Queen's Park Rangers	A 1-1	Robson
21 D1 Southampton	H 3-2	Robson, Stapleton, Muhren

February

4 D1 Norwich City	H 0-0	
7 D1 Birmingham City	A 2-2	Whiteside, Hogg
12 D1 Luton Town	A 5-0	Robson 2, Whiteside 2, Stapleton
18 D1 Wolves	A 1-1	Whiteside
25 D1 Sunderland	H 2-1	Moran 2

March

3 D1 Aston Villa	A 3-0	Moses, Whiteside, Robson
7 ECWC Barcelona	A 0-2	
10 D1 Leicester City	H 2-0	Moses, Hughes
17 D1 Arsenal	H 4-0	Muhren 2 (inc. 1 pen), Stapleton, Robson
21 ECWC Barcelona	H 3-0	Robson 2, Stapleton
31 D1 West Bromwich Albion	A 0-2	

April

7 D1 Birmingham City	H 1-0	Robson
11 ECWCSF Juventus	H 1-1	Davies
14 D1 Notts County	A 0-1	
17 D1 Watford	A 0-0	
21 D1 Coventry City	H 4-1	Hughes 2, McGrath, Wilkins
25 ECWCSF Juventus	A 1-2	Whiteside
28 D1 West Ham United	H 0-0	

May

5 D1 Everton	A 1-1	Stapleton
7 D1 Ipswich Town	H 1-2	Hughes
12 D1 Tottenham Hotspur	A 1-1	Whiteside
16 D1 Nottingham Forest	A 0-2	

Final League position: 4th

━━━━━━ **1984-85** ━━━━━━

Manager: Ron Atkinson
Played 60, **Won** 24, **Lost** 12, **Drawn** 14, **Goals for** 113, **Goals against** 62
Appearances (including as a substitute): Albiston 57; Strachan 56; Bailey, Hughes 55; Olsen 51; Robson 46; Duxbury, Hogg 43; Gidman 41; Whiteside 39; Moses 38; Stapleton 37;

McGrath 32; Moran 28; Brazil 27; Muhren 18; McQueen 15;
Garton 9; Pears 5; Blackmore 2; Davies, Graham 1
Goals: Hughes 25; Strachan 20 (inc. 7 pens); Robson 13; Brazil,
Whiteside 9 (inc. 1 pen); Stapleton 8; Olsen 6; Moran 4;
Gidman, Moses, Muhren 3 (inc. 1 pen) ; McGrath, McQueen 2;
Duxbury, own goal 1

August

25 D1 Watford	H 1-1	Strachan (pen)
28 D1 Southampton	A 0-0	

September

1 D1 Ipswich Town	A 1-1	Hughes
5 D1 Chelsea	H 1-1	Olsen
8 D1 Newcastle United	H 5-0	Hughes, Moses, Olsen, Strachan 2 (inc. 1 pen)
15 D1 Coventry City	A 3-0	Robson, Whiteside 2
19 UC Raba Vasa Eto Gyor	H 3-0	Robson, Muhren, Hughes
22 D1 Liverpool	H 1-1	Strachan (pen)
26 LC Burnley	H 4-0	Hughes 3, Robson
29 D1 West Bromwich Albion	A 2-1	Robson, Strachan (pen)

October

3 UC Raba Vasa Eto Gyor	A 2-2	Brazil, Muhren (pen)
6 D1 Aston Villa	A 0-3	
9 LC Burnley	A 3-0	Brazil 2, Olsen
13 D1 West Ham United	H 5-1	Brazil, Hughes, McQueen, Moses, Strachan
20 D1 Tottenham Hotspur	H 1-0	Hughes
24 UC PSV Eindhoven	A 0-0	
27 D1 Everton	A 0-5	
30 LC Everton	H 1-2	Brazil

November

2 D1 Arsenal	H 4-2	Hughes, Robson, Strachan 2
7 UC PSV Eindhoven	H 1-0 *(a.e.t.)*	Strachan (pen)
10 D1 Leicester City	A 3-2	Brazil, Hughes, Strachan(pen)
17 D1 Luton Town	H 2-0	Whiteside 2
24 D1 Sunderland	A 2-3	Hughes, Robson
28 UC Dundee United	H 2-2	Strachan (pen), Robson

December

1 D1 Norwich City	H 2-0	Hughes, Robson
8 D1 Nottingham Forest	A 2-3	Strachan 2 (inc. 1 pen)
12 UC Dundee United	A 3-2	Hughes, Muhren, McGinnis (o.g.)
15 D1 Queen's Park Rangers	H 3-0	Brazil, Duxbury, Gidman
22 D1 Ipswich Town	H 3-0	Gidman, Robson, Strachan (pen)
26 D1 Stoke City	A 1-2	Stapleton
29 D1 Chelsea	A 3-1	Hughes, Moses, Stapleton

January

1 D1 Sheffield Wednesday	H 1-2	Hughes
5 FA Bournemouth	H 3-0	Strachan, McQueen, Stapleton
12 D1 Coventry City	H 0-1	
26 FA Coventry City	H 2-1	Hughes, McGrath

February

2 D1 West Bromwich Albion	H 2-0	Strachan 2
9 D1 Newcastle United	A 1-1	Moran
15 FA Blackburn Rovers	H 2-0	Strachan, McGrath
23 D1 Arsenal	A 1-0	Whiteside

March

2 D1 Everton	H 1-1	Olsen
6 UC Videoton	H 1-0	Stapleton
9 FA West Ham United	H 4-2	Whiteside 3 (inc. 1 pen), Hughes
12 D1 Tottenham Hotspur	A 2-1	Hughes, Whiteside
15 D1 West Ham United	A 2-2	Robson, Stapleton

20 UC Videoton	A 0-1 *(a.e.t.)* [Videoton won 6-4 on penalties]
23 D1 Aston Villa	H 4-0	Hughes 3, Whiteside
31 D1 Liverpool	A 1-0	Stapleton

April

3 D1 Leicester City	H 2-1	Robson, Stapleton
6 D1 Stoke City	H 5-0	Hughes 2, Olsen 2, Whiteside
9 D1 Sheffield Wednesday	A 0-1	
13 FASF Liverpool	N 2-2 *(a.e.t.)*	Hughes, Stapleton
17 FASF Liverpool	N 2-1	Robson, Hughes
21 D1 Luton Town	A 1-2	Whiteside
24 D1 Southampton	H 0-0	
27 D1 Sunderland	H 2-2	Moran, Robson

May

4 D1 Norwich City	A 1-0	Moran
6 D1 Nottingham Forest	H 2-0	Gidman, Stapleton
11 D1 Queen's Park Rangers	A 3-1	Brazil 2, Strachan
13 D1 Watford	A 1-5	Moran
18 FAF Everton	W 1-0	Whiteside

Final League position: 4th
Won FA Cup

━━━━━━━━ **1985-86** ━━━━━━━━

Manger: Ron Atkinson
Played 52, **Won** 27, **Lost** 13, **Drawn** 12, **Goals for** 80, **Goals against** 42
Appearances (including as a substitute): Stapleton 51;
McGrath 49; Whiteside 47; Albiston, Hughes 46; Olsen 37;
Strachan 34; Bailey 32; Duxbury 30; Gidman 28; Robson 27;
Moran 26; C. Gibson 22; Hogg, Turner 20; Blackmore 17;
Barnes, Brazil 15; Davenport, Garton 11; Higgins 8;
T. Gibson 7; Moses 5; Sivebaek 3; Dempsey, Wood 1
Goals: Hughes 18; Olsen 13 (inc. 5 pens); Stapleton 9; Robson
(inc. 2 pens), Whiteside 7; C. Gibson, Strachan (inc. 1 pen) 5;
McGrath 4; Barnes, Blackmore, Brazil 3; Albiston,
Davenport (pen), Duxbury 1

August

10 CS Everton	W 0-2	
17 D1 Aston Villa	H 4-0	Whiteside, Hughes 2, Olsen
20 D1 Ipswich Town	A 1-0	Robson
24 D1 Arsenal	A 2-1	Hughes, McGrath
26 D1 West Ham United	H 2-0	Hughes, Strachan
31 D1 Nottingham Forest	A 3-1	Hughes, Barnes, Stapleton

September

4 D1 Newcastle United	H 3-0	Hughes, Stapleton 2
7 D1 Oxford United	H 3-0	Whiteside, Robson, Barnes
14 D1 Manchester City	A 3-0	Robson (pen), Albiston, Duxbury
21 D1 West Bromwich Albion	A 5-1	Brazil 2, Strachan, Stapleton, Blackmore
24 LC Crystal Palace	A 1-0	Barnes
28 D1 Southampton	H 1-0	Hughes

October

5 D1 Luton Town	A 1-1	Hughes
9 LC Crystal Palace	H 1-0	Whiteside
12 D1 Queen's Park Rangers	H 2-0	Hughes, Olsen
19 D1 Liverpool	H 1-1	McGrath
26 D1 Chelsea	A 2-1	Olsen, Hughes
29 LC West Ham United	H 1-0	Whiteside

November

2	D1	Coventry City	H 2-0 Olsen 2
9	D1	Sheffield Wednesday	A 0-1
16	D1	Tottenham Hotspur	H 0-0
23	D1	Leicester City	A 0-3
26	LC	Liverpool	A 1-2 McGrath
30	D1	Watford	H 1-1 Brazil

December

7	D1	Ipswich Town	H 1-0 Stapleton
14	D1	Aston Villa	A 3-1 Blackmore, Strachan, Hughes
21	D1	Arsenal	H 0-1
26	D1	Everton	A 1-3 Stapleton

January

1	D1	Birmingham City	H 1-0 C. Gibson
9	FA	Rochdale	H 2-0 Stapleton, Hughes
11	D1	Oxford United	A 3-1 Whiteside, Hughes, C. Gibson
18	D1	Nottingham Forest	H 2-3 Olsen 2 (inc. 1 pen)
25	FA	Sunderland	A 0-0
29	FAR	Sunderland	H 3-0 Olsen 2, Whiteside

February

2	D1	West Ham United	A 1-2 Robson
9	D1	Liverpool	A 1-1 C. Gibson
22	D1	West Bromwich Albion	H 3-0 Olsen 3 (inc. 2 pens)

March

1	D1	Southampton	A 0-1
5	FA	West Ham United	A 1-1 Stapleton
9	FAR	West Ham United	H 0-2
15	D1	Queen's Park Rangers	A 0-1
19	D1	Luton Town	H 2-0 Hughes, McGrath
22	D1	Manchester City	H 2-2 C. Gibson, Strachan (pen)
29	D1	Birmingham City	A 1-1 Robson
31	D1	Everton	H 0-0

April

5	D1	Coventry City	A 3-1 C. Gibson, Robson, Strachan
9	D1	Chelsea	H 1-2 Olsen (pen)
13	D1	Sheffield Wednesday	H 0-2
16	D1	Newcastle United	A 4-2 Robson (pen), Hughes 2, Whiteside
19	D1	Tottenham Hotspur	A 0-0
26	D1	Leicester City	H 4-0 Stapleton, Blackmore, Hughes, Davenport (pen)

May

3	D1	Watford	A 1-1 Hughes

Final League position: 4th

━━━━━━━ **1986-87** ━━━━━━━

Manager: Ron Atkinson and then Alex Ferguson, who took charge from the Oxford United match on 8th November 1986
Played 48, **Won** 17, **Lost** 16, **Drawn** 15, **Goals for** 61, **Goals against** 52
Appearances (including as a substitute): Davenport 45; McGrath, Stapleton 40; Moran, Strachan 38; Duxbury, Whiteside 37; Robson 33; Olsen 32; Sivebaek 31; Turner 29; Albiston, C. Gibson 26; Moses 22; T. Gibson 20; Walsh 14; Blackmore, Hogg 13; Garton, O'Brien 11; Barnes 9; Bailey 5; Wood 3; Gill 1
Goals: Davenport 16 (inc. 5 pens); Whiteside 10; Stapleton 9; Robson 7; Strachan 4; Olsen 3 (inc. 1 pen); McGrath, Moses, own goals 2; Barnes, Blackmore, Duxbury, C. Gibson, T. Gibson, Sivebaek 1

August

23	D1	Arsenal	A 0-1
25	D1	West Ham United	H 2-3 Stapleton, Davenport
30	D1	Charlton Athletic	H 0-1

September

6	D1	Leicester City	A 1-1 Whiteside
13	D1	Southampton	H 5-1 Olsen (pen), Davenport, Stapleton 2, Whiteside
16	D1	Watford	A 0-1
21	D1	Everton	A 1-3 Robson
24	LC	Port Vale	H 2-0 Stapleton, Whiteside
28	D1	Chelsea	H 0-1

October

4	D1	Nottingham Forest	A 1-1 Robson
7	LC	Port Vale	A 5-2 Moses 2, Barnes Stapleton, Davenport
11	D1	Sheffield Wednesday	H 3-1 Davenport 2 (inc. 1 pen), Whiteside
18	D1	Luton Town	H 1-0 Stapleton
26	D1	Manchester City	A 1-1 Stapleton
29	LC	Southampton	H 0-0

November

1	D1	Coventry City	H 1-1 Davenport
4	LCR	Southampton	A 1-4 Davenport
8	D1	Oxford United	A 0-2
15	D1	Norwich City	A 0-0
22	D1	Queen's Park Rangers	H 1-0 Sivebaek
29	D1	Wimbledon	A 0-1

December

7	D1	Tottenham Hotspur	H 3-3 Whiteside, Davenport 2
13	D1	Aston Villa	A 3-3 Davenport 2, Whiteside
20	D1	Leicester City	H 2-0 C. Gibson, Stapleton
26	D1	Liverpool	A 1-0 Stapleton
27	D1	Norwich City	H 0-1

January

1	D1	Newcastle United	H 4-1 Jackson (o.g.), Whiteside, Stapleton, Olsen
3	D1	Southampton	A 1-1 Olsen
10	FA	Manchester City	H 1-0 Whiteside
24	D1	Arsenal	H 2-0 Strachan, T. Gibson
31	FA	Coventry City	H 0-1

February

7	D1	Charlton Athletic	A 0-0
14	D1	Watford	H 3-1 McGrath, Strachan, Davenport (pen)
21	D1	Chelsea	A 1-1 Davenport (pen)
28	D1	Everton	H 0-0

March

7	D1	Manchester City	H 2-0 Reid (o.g.), Robson
14	D1	Luton Town	A 1-2 Robson
21	D1	Sheffield Wednesday	A 0-1
28	D1	Nottingham Forest	H 2-0 McGrath, Robson

April

4	D1	Oxford United	H 3-2 Davenport 2, Robson
14	D1	West Ham United	A 0-0
18	D1	Newcastle United	A 1-2 Strachan
20	D1	Liverpool	H 1-0 Davenport
25	D1	Queen's Park Rangers	A 1-1 Strachan

May

2	D1	Wimbledon	H 0-1
4	D1	Tottenham Hotspur	A 0-4
6	D1	Coventry City	A 1-1 Whiteside
9	D1	Aston Villa	H 3-1 Blackmore, Duxbury, Robson

Final League position: 11th

1987-88

Manager: Alex Ferguson
Played 48, **Won** 29, **Lost** 7, **Drawn** 12, **Goals for** 86, **Goals against** 40
Appearances (including as a substitute): McClair 48; Duxbury 47; Olsen, Strachan 44; Robson 43; Davenport 40; Anderson 38; C. Gibson 36; Whiteside 35; Turner 30; Blackmore 28; Bruce, McGrath, Moran 24; O'Brien 21; Moses 20; Walsh 18; Hogg 13; Albiston 11; Garton 9; Graham 2; Martin 1
Goals: McClair 31 (inc. 6 pens); Robson 11; Whiteside 10; Strachan 9; Davenport 6; Anderson, Blackmore, McGrath 3; Bruce, C. Gibson, O'Brien, Olsen, own goals 2

August
15 D1 Southampton	A 2-2	Whiteside 2
19 D1 Arsenal	H 0-0	
22 D1 Watford	H 2-0	McGrath, McClair
29 D1 Charlton Athletic	A 3-1	McGrath, McClair, Robson
31 D1 Chelsea	H 3-1	McClair, Strachan, Whiteside

September
5 D1 Coventry City	A 0-0	
12 D1 Newcastle United	H 2-2	Olsen, McClair (pen)
19 D1 Everton	A 1-2	Whiteside
23 LC Hull City	H 5-0	Whiteside, Strachan, McGrath, McClair, Davenport
26 D1 Tottenham Hotspur	H 1-0	McClair (pen)

October
3 D1 Luton Town	A 1-1	McClair
7 LC Hull City	A 1-0	McClair
10 D1 Sheffield Wednesday	A 4-2	Robson, McClair 2, Blackmore
17 D1 Norwich City	H 2-1	Davenport, Robson
25 D1 West Ham United	A 1-1	C. Gibson
28 LC Crystal Palace	H 2-1	McClair 2

November
15 D1 Liverpool	H 1-1	Whiteside
18 LC Bury	H 2-1	Whiteside, McClair
21 D1 Wimbledon	A 1-2	Blackmore

December
5 D1 Queen's Park Rangers	A 2-0	Davenport, Robson
12 D1 Oxford United	H 3-1	Strachan 2, Olsen
19 D1 Portsmouth	A 2-1	Robson, McClair
26 D1 Newcastle United	A 0-1	
28 D1 Everton	H 2-1	McClair 2 (inc. 1 pen)

January
1 D1 Charlton Athletic	H 0-0	
2 D1 Watford	A 1-0	McClair
10 FA Ipswich Town	A 2-1	D'Avray (o.g.), Anderson
16 D1 Southampton	H 0-2	
20 LC Oxford United	A 0-2	
24 D1 Arsenal	A 2-1	Strachan, McClair
30 FA Chelsea	H 2-0	Whiteside, McClair

February
6 D1 Coventry City	H 1-0	O'Brien
10 D1 Derby County	A 2-1	Whiteside, Strachan
13 D1 Chelsea	A 2-1	Bruce, O'Brien
20 FA Arsenal	A 1-2	McClair
23 D1 Tottenham Hotspur	A 1-1	McClair

March
5 D1 Norwich City	A 0-1	
12 D1 Sheffield Wednesday	H 4-1	Blackmore, McClair 2, Davenport

BOUGHT
1:	Viv Anderson	from Arsenal	for £250,000
2:	Brian McClair	from Celtic	for £850,000
3:	Steve Bruce	from Norwich City	for £825,000
4:	Paul Dalton	from Brandon	for £5000
5:	Lee Sharpe	from Torquay	for £180,000
6:	Jim Leighton	from Aberdeen	for £750,000
7:	Mark Hughes	from Barcelona	for £1.8 m
8:	Mal Donaghy	from Luton Town	for £750,000
9:	Ralph Milne	from Bristol City	for £175,000
10:	G. Maiorana	from Histon	for £30,000
11:	Neil Webb	from Nott'm Forest	for £1.5 m
12:	Michael Phelan	from Norwich City	for £750,000
13:	Brian Carey	from Cork City	for £100,000
14:	Gary Pallister	from Middlesbrough	for £2.3 m
15:	Paul Ince	from West Ham Utd	for £800,000
16:	Danny Wallace	from Southampton	for £1.2 m
17:	Andy Rammell	from Atherstone Utd	for £20,000
18:	Denis Irwin	from Oldham Ath.	for £650,000
19:	Neil Whitworth	from Wigan Athletic	for £80,000
20:	A. Kanchelskis	from Shak. Donetsk	for £650,0000
21:	Peter Schmeichel	from Brondby	for £750,000
22:	Paul Parker	from QPR	for £1.8 m

SOLD
1:	Fraser Digby	to Swindon Town	for £25,000
2:	Peter Barnes	to Manchester City	for £15,500
3:	Mark Higgins	to Bury	for £10,000
4:	Simon Ratcliffe	to Norwich City	for £40,000
5:	Frank Stapleton	to Ajax	free transfer
6:	Kevin Moran	to Sporting Gijon	free transfer
7:	Arthur Albiston	to West Brom	free transfer
8:	Terry Gibson	to Wimbledon	for £200,000
9:	John Sivebaek	to AS St-Etienne	for £227,000
10:	Graeme Hogg	to Portsmouth	for £150,000
11:	Chris Turner	to Sheffield Wed.	for £175,000
12:	Peter Davenport	to Middlesbrough	for £700,000
13:	Liam O'Brien	to Newcastle United	for £275,000
14:	Jesper Olsen	to Bordeaux	for £375,000
15:	Gordon Strachan	to Leeds United	for £300,000
16:	Paul Dalton	to Hartlepool Utd	for £5000
17:	Paul McGrath	to Aston Villa	for £400,000
18:	N. Whiteside	to Everton	for £750,000
19:	Wayne Heseltine	to Oldham Ath.	for £40,000
20:	Sean Goater	to Rotherham Utd	for £30,000
21:	Mike Duxbury	to Blackburn Rovers	free transfer
21:	Andrew Rammell	to Barnsley	for £100,000
23:	Colin Gibson	to Leicester City	for £120,000
24:	Viv Anderson	to Sheffield Wed.	free transfer
25:	Wayne Bullimore	to Barnsley	free transfer
26:	Les Sealey	to Aston Villa	for £250,000
27:	Deiniol Graham	to Barnsley	free transfer
28:	David Wilson	to Bristol Rovers	free transfer
29:	Jim Leighton	to Dundee United	for £250,000
29:	Mark Bosnich	to Aston Villa	for £70,000
30:	Jason Lydiate	to Bolton Wanderers	free transfer
31:	Sean McAuley	to Saint Johnstone	£100,000

Total spent = £16,215,000
Total received = £4,607,500

19 D1 Nottingham Forest	A 0-0	
26 D1 West Ham United	H 3-1 Strachan, Anderson, Robson	

April

2 D1 Derby County	H 4-1 McClair 3, C. Gibson
4 D1 Liverpool	A 3-3 Robson 2, Strachan
12 D1 Luton Town	H 3-0 McClair, Robson, Davenport
30 D1 Queen's Park Rangers	H 2-1 Bruce, Parker (o.g.)

May

2 D1 Oxford United	A 2-0 Anderson, Strachan
7 D1 Portsmouth	H 4-1 McClair 2 (inc. 1 pen), Davenport, Robson
9 D1 Wimbledon	H 2-1 McClair 2 (inc. 1 pen)

Final League position: 2nd

1988-89

Manager Alex Ferguson
Played 48, **Won** 18, **Lost** 15, **Drawn** 15, **Goals for** 62, **Goals against** 41
Appearances (including as a substitute): Bruce, Hughes, Leighton, McClair 48; Robson 43; Blackmore, Donaghy 37; Beardsmore, Sharpe 30; Martin, Milne, Strachan 29; McGrath 26; Duxbury 21; Garton 16; Gill 13; Olsen 12; Robins, Davenport 10; Anderson 7; Maiorana, Whiteside, Wilson 6, O'Brien, C. Gibson 3; D. Brazil, Graham 1
Goals: Hughes, McClair 16 (inc. 1 pen); Robson 8; Bruce 4; Blackmore, Davenport, Milne 3; Beardsmore, Gill, own goals 2; Graham, Martin, McGrath, Strachan 1

August

27 D1 Queen's Park Rangers	H 0-0

September

3 D1 Liverpool	A 0-1
10 D1 Middlesbrough	H 1-0 Robson
17 D1 Luton Town	A 2-0 Davenport, Robson
24 D1 West Ham United	H 2-0 Davenport, Hughes
28 LC Rotherham United	A 1-0 Davenport

October

1 D1 Tottenham Hotspur	A 2-2 Hughes, McClair
12 LC Rotherham United	H 5-0 McClair 3, Robson, Bruce
22 D1 Wimbledon	A 1-1 Hughes
26 D1 Norwich City	H 1-2 Hughes
30 D1 Everton	A 1-1 Hughes

November

2 LC Wimbledon	A 1-2 Robson
5 D1 Aston Villa	H 1-1 Bruce
12 D1 Derby County	A 2-2 Hughes, McClair
19 D1 Southampton	H 2-2 Robson, Hughes
23 D1 Sheffield Wednesday	H 1-1 Hughes
27 D1 Newcastle United	A 0-0

December

3 D1 Charlton Athletic	H 3-0 Milne, McClair, Hughes
10 D1 Coventry City	A 0-1
17 D1 Arsenal	A 1-2 Hughes
26 D1 Nottingham Forest	H 2-0 Milne, Hughes

January

1 D1 Liverpool	H 3-1 McClair, Hughes, Beardsmore
2 D1 Middlesbrough	A 0-1
7 FA Queen's Park Rangers	H 0-0
11 FAR Queen's Park Rangers	A 2-2 *(a.e.t.)* Gill, Graham
14 D1 Millwall	H 3-0 Blackmore, Gill, Hughes

21 D1 West Ham United	A 3-1 Strachan, Martin, McClair
23 FAR Queen's Park Rangers	H 3-0 McClair 2 (inc. 1 pen), Robson
28 FA Oxford United	H 4-0 Hughes, Bruce, Phillips (o.g.), Robson

February

5 D1 Tottenham Hotspur	H 1-0 McClair
11 D1 Sheffield Wednesday	A 2-0 McClair 2
18 FA Bournemouth	A 1-1 Hughes
22 FAR Bournemouth	H 1-0 McClair
25 D1 Norwich City	A 1-2 McGrath

March

12 D1 Aston Villa	A 0-0
18 FA Nottingham Forest	H 0-1
25 D1 Luton Town	H 2-0 Milne, Blackmore
27 D1 Nottingham Forest	A 0-2

April

2 D1 Arsenal	H 1-1 Adams (o.g.)
8 D1 Millwall	A 0-0
15 D1 Derby County	H 0-2
22 D1 Charlton Athletic	A 0-1
29 D1 Coventry City	H 0-1

May

2 D1 Wimbledon	H 1-0 McClair
6 D1 Southampton	A 1-2 Beardsmore
8 D1 Queen's Park Rangers	A 2-3 Bruce, Blackmore
10 D1 Everton	H 1-2 Hughes
13 D1 Newcastle United	H 2-0 McClair, Robson

Final League position: 11th

1989-90

Manager: Alex Ferguson
Played 49, **Won** 20, **Lost** 17, **Drawn** 12, **Goals for** 64, **Goals against** 61
Appearances (including as a substitute): Hughes, McClair, Phelan 48; Pallister 46; Leighton 45; Bruce 43; Martin 41; Ince 36; Wallace 35; Blackmore 31; Robson 27; Beardsmore, Duxbury 25; Robins 23; Anderson 21; Sharpe 20; Donaghy 18; Webb 15; C. Gibson 8; Sealey 3; Maiorana 2; Bosnich, Brazil, Graham, Milne 1
Goals: Hughes 15; Robins, McClair 8; Wallace 6; Robson 4; Blackmore, Bruce (inc. 1 pen), Pallister, Webb 3; Beardsmore, Ince 2; Gibson, Martin, own goal, Phelan, Sharpe 1

August

19 D1 Arsenal	H 4-1 Bruce, Hughes, Webb, McClair
22 D1 Crystal Palace	A 1-1 Robson
26 D1 Derby County	A 0-2
30 D1 Norwich City	H 0-2

September

9 D1 Everton	A 2-3 Beardsmore, McClair
16 D1 Millwall	H 5-1 Hughes 3, Robson, Sharpe
20 LC Portsmouth	A 3-2 Ince 2, Wallace
23 D1 Manchester City	A 1-5 Hughes

October

3 LC Portsmouth	H 0-0
14 D1 Sheffield Wednesday	H 0-0
21 D1 Coventry City	A 4-1 Bruce, Hughes 2, Phelan
25 D1 Tottenham Hotspur	H 0-3
28 D1 Southampton	H 2-1 McClair 2

November

4 D1 Charlton Athletic	A 0-2
12 D1 Nottingham Forest	H 1-0 Pallister

18 D1 Luton Town A 3-1 Wallace, Blackmore, Hughes

25 D1 Chelsea H 0-0

December

3 D1 Arsenal A 0-1

9 D1 Crystal Palace H 1-2 Beardsmore

16 D1 Tottenham Hotspur H 0-1

23 D1 Liverpool A 0-0

26 D1 Aston Villa A 0-3

30 D1 Wimbledon A 2-2 Hughes, Robins

January

1 D1 Queen's Park Rangers H 0-0

7 FA Nottingham Forest A 1-0 Robins

13 D1 Derby County H 1-2 Pallister

21 D1 Norwich City A 0-2

28 FA Hereford United A 1-0 Blackmore

February

3 D1 Manchester City H 1-1 Blackmore

10 D1 Millwall A 2-1 Wallace, Hughes

18 FA Newcastle United A 3-2 Robins, Wallace, McClair

24 D1 Chelsea A 0-1

March

3 D1 Luton Town H 4-1 McClair, Hughes, Wallace, Robins

11 FA Sheffield United A 1-0 McClair

14 D1 Everton H 0-0

18 D1 Liverpool H 1-2 Whelan (o.g.)

21 D1 Sheffield Wednesday A 0-1

24 D1 Southampton A 2-0 C. Gibson, Robins

31 D1 Coventry City H 3-0 Hughes 2, Robins

April

8 FASF Oldham Athletic N 3-3 *(a.e.t.)* Robson, Webb, Wallace

11 FASFR Oldham Athletic N 2-1 *(a.e.t.)* McClair, Robins

14 D1 Queen's Park Rangers A 2-1 Robins, Webb

17 D1 Aston Villa H 2-0 Robins 2

21 D1 Tottenham Hotspur A 1-2 Bruce (pen)

30 D1 Wimbledon H 0-0

May

2 D1 Nottingham Forest A 0-4

5 D1 Charlton Athletic H 1-0 Pallister

12 FAF Crystal Palace W 3-3 *(a.e.t.)* Hughes 2, Robson

17 FAFR Crystal Palace W 1-0 Martin

Final League position: 13th **Won FA Cup**

━━━━━━ **1990-91** ━━━━━━

Manager: Alex Ferguson

Played 60, **Won** 32, **Lost** 12, **Drawn** 16 **Goals for** 101, **Goals against** 63

Appearances (including as a substitute): Pallister 59; McClair 58; Blackmore 57; Hughes, Irwin 53; Sealey 52; Bruce, Phelan 51; Ince 48; Webb 47; Sharpe 42; Donaghy 38; Robson 30; Wallace 29; Robins 27; Martin 25; Beardsmore 15; Walsh 6; Ferguson 5; Anderson 3; Giggs, Wratten 2; Bosnich, Kanchelskis, Leighton, Whitworth 1

Goals: Hughes, McClair 21; Bruce 19 (inc. 11 pens); Blackmore, Sharpe 9; Robins, Webb 5; Wallace 4; Ince 3; Anderson, Giggs, Pallister, Phelan, Robson 1

August

18 CS Liverpool W 1-1 Blackmore

25 D1 Coventry City H 2-0 Bruce, Webb

28 D1 Leeds United A 0-0

September

1 D1 Sunderland A 1-2 McClair

4 D1 Luton Town A 1-0 Robins

8 D1 Queen's Park Rangers H 3-1 Robins 2, McClair

16 D1 Liverpool A 0-4

19 ECWC Pecsi Munkas H 2-0 Blackmore, Webb

22 D1 Southampton H 3-2 McClair, Hughes, Blackmore

26 LC Halifax Town A 3-1 Blackmore, McClair, Webb

29 D1 Nottingham Forest H 0-1

October

3 ECWC Pecsi Munkas A 1-0 McClair

10 LC Halifax Town H 2-1 Anderson, Bruce (pen)

20 D1 Arsenal H 0-1

23 ECWC Wrexham H 3-0 Bruce (pen), McClair, Pallister

27 D1 Manchester City A 3-3 Hughes, McClair 2

31 LC Liverpool H 3-1 Bruce (pen), Hughes, Sharpe

November

3 D1 Crystal Palace H 2-0 Webb, Wallace

7 ECWC Wrexham A 2-0 Bruce, Robins

10 D1 Derby County A 0-0

17 D1 Sheffield United H 2-0 Hughes, Bruce

25 D1 Chelsea H 2-3 Hughes, Wallace

28 LC Arsenal A 6-2 Blackmore, Hughes, Sharpe 3, Wallace

December

1 D1 Everton A 1-0 Sharpe

8 D1 Leeds United H 1-1 Webb

15 D1 Coventry City A 2-2 Hughes, Wallace

22 D1 Wimbledon A 3-1 Bruce 2 (inc. 2 pens) Hughes

26 D1 Norwich City H 3-0 McClair 2, Hughes

29 D1 Aston Villa H 1-1 Bruce (pen)

January

1 D1 Tottenham Hotspur A 2-1 Bruce (pen), McClair

7 FA Queen's Park Rangers H 2-1 Hughes, McClair

12 D1 Sunderland H 3-0 Hughes 2, McClair

16 LC Southampton A 1-1 Hughes

19 D1 Queen's Park Rangers A 1-1 Phelan

23 LCR Southampton H 3-2 Hughes 3

26 FA Bolton Wanderers H 1-0 Hughes

February

3 D1 Liverpool H 1-1 Bruce (pen)

10 LCSF Leeds United H 2-1 Sharpe, McClair

18 FA Norwich City A 1-2 McClair

24 LCSF Leeds United A 1-0 Sharpe

26 D1 Sheffield United A 1-2 Blackmore (pen)

March

2 D1 Everton H 0-2

6 ECWC Montpellier H 1-1 McClair

9 D1 Chelsea A 2-3 Hughes, McClair

13 D1 Southampton A 1-1 Ince

16 D1 Nottingham Forest A 1-1 Blackmore

19 ECWC Montpellier A 2-0 Blackmore, Bruce (pen)

23 D1 Luton Town H 4-1 Bruce 2, Robins, McClair

30 D1 Norwich City A 3-0 Bruce 2 (inc. 1 pen), Ince

April

2 D1 Wimbledon H 2-1 Bruce, McClair

6 D1 Aston Villa A 1-1 Sharpe

10 ECWCSF Legia Warsaw A 3-1 McClair, Hughes, Bruce

16 D1 Derby County H 3-1 Blackmore, McClair, Robson

21 LCF Sheffield Wednesday W 0-1

24 ECWCSF Legia Warsaw H 1-1 Sharpe

May

4 D1 Manchester City	H 1-0 Giggs
6 D1 Arsenal	A 1-3 Bruce (pen)
11 D1 Crystal Palace	A 0-3
15 ECWCF Barcelona	N 2-1 Hughes 2
20 D1 Tottenham Hotspur	H 1-1 Ince

Final League position: 6th
Won European Cup Winners' Cup
Finalists Rumbelows League Cup

━━━━━━━━━━ **1991-92** ━━━━━━━━━━

Manager: Alex Ferguson
Played 58, **Won** 30, **Lost** 7, **Drawn** 21, **Goals for** 86, **Goals against** 44
Appearances (including as a substitute): McClair 58; Pallister 56; Hughes, Schmeichel 53; Giggs, Irwin 51; Bruce 50; Ince 47; Webb 43; Kanchelskis 41; Blackmore 40; Robson 38; Parker, 37; Donaghy 26; Phelan 25; Sharpe 20; Robins 8; Martin 6; Ferguson, Walsh 4; Beardsmore 3; Wallace 2; Wilkinson 1
Goals: McClair 26; Hughes 14; Giggs, Kanchelskis 7; Bruce (inc. 3 pens) 6; Robson 5; Blackmore (inc. 1 pen), Ince, Irwin 4; Webb 3; Robins, Sharpe 2; Pallister, own goal 1

August

17 D1 Notts County	H 2-0 Hughes, Robson
21 D1 Aston Villa	A 1-0 Bruce (pen)
24 D1 Everton	A 0-0
28 D1 Oldham Athletic	H 1-0 McClair
31 D1 Leeds United	H 1-1 Robson

September

3 D1 Wimbledon	A 2-1 Pallister, Blackmore
7 D1 Norwich City	H 3-0 Irwin, Giggs, McClair
14 D1 Southampton Town	A 1-0 Hughes
18 ECWC Athinaikos	A 0-0
21 D1 Luton Town	H 5-0 McClair 2, Bruce (pen), Ince, Hughes
25 LC Cambridge United	H 3-0 Bruce, McClair, Giggs
28 D1 Tottenham Hotspur	A 2-1 Hughes, Robson

October

2 ECWC Athinaikos	H 2-0 (a.e.t.) Hughes, McClair
6 D1 Liverpool	H 0-0
9 LC Cambridge United	A 1-1 McClair
19 D1 Arsenal	H 1-1 Bruce
23 ECWC Atletico Madrid	A 0-3
26 D1 Sheffield Wednesday	A 2-3 McClair 2
30 LC Portsmouth	H 3-1 Robins 2, Robson

November

2 D1 Sheffield United	H 2-0 McClair, Hoyland o.g.
6 ECWC Atletico Madrid	H 1-1 Hughes
16 D1 Manchester City	A 0-0
19 ESC Red Star Belgrade	H 1-0 McClair
23 D1 West Ham United	H 2-1 Robson, Giggs
30 D1 Crystal Palace	A 3-1 Kanchelskis, Webb, McClair

December

4 LC Oldham Athletic	H 2-0 McClair, Kanchelskis
7 D1 Coventry City	H 4-0 Bruce, Webb, McClair, Hughes
15 D1 Chelsea	A 3-1 Irwin, Bruce (pen), McClair

26 D1 Oldham Athletic	A 6-3 Irwin 2, McClair 2, Kanchelskis, Giggs
29 D1 Leeds United	A 1-1 Webb

January

1 D1 Queen's Park Rangers	H 1-4 McClair
8 LC Leeds United	A 3-1 Blackmore, Giggs, Kanchelskis
11 D1 Everton	H 1-0 Kanchelskis
15 FA Leeds United	A 1-0 Hughes
18 D1 Notts County	A 1-1 Blackmore (pen)
22 D1 Aston Villa	H 1-0 Hughes
27 FA Southampton	A 0-0

February

1 D1 Arsenal	A 1-1 McClair
4 FAR Southampton	H 2-2 (a.e.t.) McClair, Kanchelskis
	[Southampton won 4-2 on penalties]
8 D1 Sheffield Wednesday	H 1-1 McClair
22 D1 Crystal Palace	H 2-0 Hughes 2
26 D1 Chelsea	H 1-1 Hughes
29 D1 Coventry City	A 0-0

March

4 LCSF Middlesbrough	A 0-0
11 LCSF Middlesbrough	H 2-1 (a.e.t) Sharpe, Giggs
14 D1 Sheffield United	A 2-1 McClair, Blackmore
18 D1 Nottingham Forest	A 0-1
21 D1 Wimbledon	H 0-0
28 D1 Queen's Park Rangers	A 0-0
31 D1 Norwich City	A 3-1 Ince (2), McClair

April

7 D1 Manchester City	H 1-1 Giggs
12 LCF Nottingham Forest	W 1-0 McClair
16 D1 Southampton	H 1-0 Kanchelskis
18 D1 Luton Town	A 1-1 Sharpe
20 D1 Nottingham Forest	H 1-2 McClair
22 D1 West Ham United	A 0-1
26 D1 Liverpool	A 0-2

May

2 D1 Tottenham Hotspur	H 3-1 McClair, Hughes (2)

Final League position: 2nd Won Rumbelows League Cup
Won European Super Cup

TOP TEN POSTWAR APPEARANCES

1: Bobby Charlton: *754 games, 247 goals*

2: Bill Foulkes, *682 games, 9 goals*

3: Alex Stepney, *535 games, 2 goals*

3: Tony Dunne, *530 games, 2 goals*

4: Arthur Albiston, *482 games, 7 goals*

5: George Best, *466 games, 178 goals*

6: Martin Buchan, *455 games, 4 goals*

7: Jack Rowley, *422 games, 208 goals*

8: Sammy McIlroy, *418 games, 70 goals*

9: Bryan Robson, *411 games, 93 goals*

10: Lou Macari, *400 games, 97 goals*

INDEX

Please note that entries in **bold** refer to captions